INTRODUCTION TO
SIGNS AND WONDERS

Augusto Perez

INTRODUCTION TO SIGN AND WONDERS
ISBN-13: 9780967847306

Published by:
Augusto L. Perez

For information on bookings or to place an order please contact us at:

The Appearance Ministries, Inc.
P.O. Box 465
Live Oak, FL. 32064
Web Address: www.theappearance.com
Email: augusto@theappearance.com

Printed in the United States
First Printing: 2000
Second Printing: 2006 by Morris Publishing
3212 East Highway 30
Kearney, NE 68847
1-800-650-7888

DEDICATION

I dedicate this book to my son Benjamin (*Son of the Right Hand*), and to my daughter Charis (*Grace*), the two treasures the Lord has given us. May you live up to the potential blessings and promises inherent in your names, and may the God of Abraham, Isaac and Jacob bless you and grant you long and prosperous lives.

Your mother and I are blessed
to have you. We love you.

ACKNOWLEDGEMENTS

I want to thank my Father and Lord Jesus Christ, whom I love
with all my heart, and the precious Holy Spirit. Thank you
for helping and inspiring me to write this book;
I could never have done it without you.
I need you!

To my wife Yvette for understanding the call God has placed
upon my life and releasing me to go and fulfill the
commission the Lord has given me.
I love you!

To all the pastors and churches that support our crusades
and are connected to our ministry.
I value you!

To all our friends who support this ministry with their gifts,
so we can continue winning souls for the Lord and
training and equipping the body of Christ.
I thank you!

TABLE OF CONTENTS

PREFACE

There is nothing more tragic than to see the people of God living their lives devoid of the presence and power of God, believing that is the norm. It is sad to see churches that have gotten so used to having services without the manifest presence of God and the intervention of the Holy Spirit, that if God removed His Spirit from their midst, they would have a hard time telling the difference.

There is no shortage of skeptics and critics who continually take poke shots at the few who lay down their lives and are bold enough to exercise their faith and manifest the power and the glory of God on the earth. To these cynical intellectual people, the supernatural power of God and signs and wonders are nothing more than extreme, unnecessary emotional outbursts of uncultured, ignorant people who need a place to vent their frustrations and help them cope with their personal problems in life.

These cotton candy, user friendly, people pleasing *"preachers"*, who are no more than shrewd administrators, businessmen and eloquent entertainers; who are quick to criticize, judge and ridicule the power of God and those who have paid the price and forsaken everything to follow the Lamb and manifest His glory, speak evil of things they know not of, and are the same ones that Jude calls waterless clouds, fruitless trees and wandering stars (Jude 1:12).

Yet, a distant rumbling is being heard by those servants to whom God, in His divine sovereignty, has chosen to reveal it to. Perhaps the sound of the approaching storm, an outpouring of the Spirit of such dramatic proportions that will cause the greatest ingathering of souls this world has ever seen. This period will coincide with increasing turbulent times and horrible events that will cause the courage of many to falter. Millions will flock to the churches seeking help for multitudes of needs, but the church in its present condition cannot handle what is coming.

These are just some of the reasons why I wrote this book. I am only one of many God is raising up at this time to speak out and bring clarity to some important areas that have been ignored, rejected and neglected by the present day church leadership. The ministries of the apostle and prophet, which are being restored to their original place and function in the church, will bring healing and restoration to the Bride of Christ preparing her to take her rightful place in the world, as the glory of God is manifested on the earth. As this army of remnant believers is raised up, trained, prepared and released into the great harvest, a revival of gigantic proportions will take place, sweeping masses of people into the kingdom of God. The transformation of the church from its present condition will be astounding.

This New Wine of the Holy Spirit will not be poured into old, dry, cracked wineskins. They cannot contain what the Lord wants to give them. This necessitates the formation of new wineskins and the reformation of old ones. This is going to require that pastors start shifting their thinking from a sermon mindset to a training mindset. Pastors alone cannot do this training. That is why Ephesians 4:11-16 mentions five ministries that the Lord uses to equip and train the saints.

I understand that not every pastor or leader is ready and willing to step into what the Lord is doing. Many are afraid, confused, lacking understanding of what to do and how to do it. There is a lot of distrust among five-fold ministries. There may be some pride and jealousy involved that makes things more difficult. Pastors do not trust prophets, and think of them as radical and strange, as many churches have been hurt before; prophets do not trust pastors, seeing them as dogmatic and controlling, having been hurt and rejected by them.

We are creatures of habits and old habits are very hard to break. After all, what worked for the last twenty years should work today, right? Wrong. Change is not comfortable but necessary, and involves a long process of adjustment, correction and reform in our lifestyles, but especially in the way we think about church. We are in the middle of an apostolic reformation, a paradigm shift that will redefine our concept of what Church is. In times past every time God was about to do something new, it necessitated a change, a re-formation in the structure (wineskin) of the existing system or church (Luke 5:37).

Apostles and prophets are an integral part of the training that must take place in the local church in these last days in order to receive the coming outpouring of

God's Holy Spirit. Many pastors are truly apostolic but are still operating under a pastoral anointing. They too must be willing to be trained and developed to step into the apostolic anointing God has for them. It is not enough for one man to operate in supernatural signs and wonders, the prophetic and deliverance anymore. The Lord wants His whole Church to be able to flow in this way. In order to do this, the foundation of the local church needs to be re-structured and re-formed. Two years ago God gave us the mandate to begin training the leaders and saints in churches here and overseas.

A wineskin or structure that was once acceptable is now being replaced by a new one that will allow us to receive the coming outpouring and reap the harvest of souls. Right now the Lord is releasing new blueprints that are being implemented in many churches in the Kingdom of God. The blueprints are being designed and released by apostles and prophets under divine inspiration and in accordance to God's Word for the benefit of the Church.

The Church was ordained by the Lord to be the spiritual scaffold whereby His body is taught, trained, discipled and then released into their callings and ministries by the presbytery of the local church. Churches need to be spiritually connected with true apostles and prophets that can be part of the local church presbytery and release the anointings and ministries in the house.

Pastors and church leaders need to lay aside personal agendas and desires, suspicions, fear, jealousies, doubts and unbelief and try to work together giving God a chance to do whatever He wants to do, with whoever He wants to use, in whatever way He desires to do it. We need to be flexible and willing to try new methods, ideas and things even if at first we don't like them or believe they won't work. We need to change some of the ways we do things, conduct services, and use ministries.

We are living in a time when the consciousness of the believers needs to be raised to a higher level where they are able to understand their role and purpose in God's kingdom, and then trained and released to operate in it. On the other hand, pastors need to understand that it is a corruption of the Body of Jesus Christ to just have believers sitting in the churches doing nothing, while the pastor or some visiting minister does all the ministry. God is now releasing the end-time ministries to prepare and train the body of Christ and set it in place so it is able to operate as it should. This will require the gathering of apostles, prophets, pastors, evangelists and teachers to have open and honest discussions about some real issues we are facing and different ways to resolve them.

We are in a transitional period of change right now and we are looking through a glass darkly. The Church Age is coming to a close as we are entering the dispensation of the Kingdom Age, where Jesus will return to establish His millennial Kingdom on the earth. Horrible events are about to take place, but an unseen hand is holding back the storm a while longer for some reason.

God is bestowing upon mankind a last act grace, a sovereign move of His Holy Spirit upon all mankind; a last chance to heed His call; earth's last opportunity, God's last call. Can a world that has rejected God, and is rushing head on into judgment expect to see revival fires? Strange as it may seem, the greatest revivals and reformations have always come at the darkest hour.

The rain of the Spirit has fallen at different times intermittently until now, but the Lord has reserved the best wine for last. More people have been saved and converted to Christianity in the last decade than in the previous two thousand years combined. A church within a church is rising up; a remnant group of believers that were hidden for a season, while they were being trained and tested in the fires of affliction. These dread warriors will make the powers of darkness tremble, turning the world upside down as the harvest of souls takes place.

These are the Moses and Elijah Company (apostles and prophets) that the Bible prophesied would appear on earth prior to the Day of the Lord. They will carry upon them the true anointing, power and authority of God. Their seal of authenticity will be their humility, compassion and godly wisdom. They will be loved by those who love righteousness and justice, but dreaded and hated by the religious and the corrupt. They will purge sin from Zion and cause the fear of the Lord to come upon people, while they also heal and restore the body of Christ (Malachi 4:1-6).

INTRODUCTION

"Truly the signs of an apostle were done among you in all patience, in signs, and wonders, and mighty deeds" (2 Corinthians 12:12). God has always used miracles, signs and wonders to distinguish a person, a thing, or event from others. These supernatural signs are His signature attesting to the authenticity of a ministry or message as was the case with the apostle Paul. Signs and wonders are foundational to the Christian faith and desperately needed in the church today. The gospel of the Lord Jesus Christ is supposed to be preached with signs and wonders following, as it was in the early church. Signs and wonders are for the unbelievers; they do not save, but they cause people to pay attention to and obey the gospel of Jesus Christ.

If there ever was a preacher who could have been successful without signs and wonders, it was Jesus. He was not only a great leader, but an eloquent, compassionate teacher. Yet when the apostle Peter referred to Jesus in Acts 2, he used miracles, signs and wonders to describe God's stamp of approval upon His life and ministry. Jesus was known for the signs, wonders and miracles that followed Him. Another preacher who could have had a great ministry without signs and wonders was the apostle Paul, yet we see in 1 Corinthians 2:4 that he summarizes and describes his ministry as one of demonstration of the spirit and of power.

There is a divine call from the throne of God to all believers to come out of their comfort zones, and allow God to use them to manifest the kingdom of God on the earth. The first step to accomplish this is to understand that you have gifts and talents from God which He expects you to develop and use to bless others in this world. One of the names the Bible calls the Church is *the Body of Christ,* meaning that it is composed of many different parts functioning together to achieve God's will upon the earth. Christians were never intended to be mere spectators who come to church once a week to hear a sermon, and watch one man do the entire ministry.

The word *ministry,* as written in Romans 12:7, means *service.* In other words, if you have received a ministry of service, you should exercise that gift in the service of other people. In the Christian circles, ministry has been equated with standing behind the pulpit and preaching the Word of God. In other groups, the ministry is allowed to pray for the needs of the people right there in the church. And even in smaller groups, people are allowed to exercise the gifts of the Holy Spirit in the church.

The ministry of Romans 12:7 and Ephesians 4:12 should not be confused with the ascension gifts of Ephesians 4:11, namely apostles, prophets, pastors, evangelists, and teachers. These were given to perfect the church saints for the work of the ministry (service), for the edifying of the body of Christ. When we see divine healing and the gifts of the Spirit as part of the normal life of believers, we are set free from elevating one person above another. Seen in this light, healing prayer is simply a way of showing God's love to people.

Healings, physical and otherwise, are the natural outflow of compassion. Scripture teaches us that God is all-loving, all-powerful, and all-healing. He takes delight in His people preferring that people be healthy, rather than sick. God demonstrated His nature best through Jesus, who was full of grace and truth. Jesus went about doing good, healing the sick, casting out devils, feeding the hungry, tearing down the kingdom of Satan, and establishing the kingdom of God upon the earth. After we are saved, we are to be conformed to the image of Jesus Christ. That means that we are supposed to change and become more and more like Him; act like Him, think like Him, and talk like Him (2 Corinthians 3:18).

We are called to manifest the love of God in this world, and to share the Good News of the Gospel. What better way to manifest the love of God than to heal the sick, set people free from the powers of darkness, feed the hungry and clothe the naked? This is done best when you allow God to use you through the power of His Spirit. As you make yourself available to Him, His love will flow through you in the form of the gifts of the Holy Spirit. Jesus embodied the kingdom of God, saving and healing people. He also trained His disciples to heal, and to operate in the power of His Spirit, that they might effectively advance the kingdom of God (Luke 9:1-11; 10:1-24 and Mark 16:14-20).

During the first hundred years of the church, healing was a common activity in Christian life. In fact, signs and wonders help explain the remarkable growth of Christianity during this period. One of the reasons for praying for the sick is that healing aids the evangelism of souls. It is a *gospel advancer* as reported by third world Christian churches that have experienced staggering church and spiritual growth in the last several years. It is easier to pray for people's healing than to tell them about Christ. In fact, it is reported from third world countries that it is easier to tell people about Jesus after they have been healed. This is verified by the Scriptures. Notice how Jesus frequently first healed the sick, then proclaimed the gospel of the kingdom of God.

Most Christians are hesitant, even fearful to pray for other people to be healed because they misunderstand God's compassion and mercy. The goal of the church is to produce mature Christians who are like Jesus, and who do the same works that He did. This can only be accomplished when each of the ministries learns to focus on its own job, without trying to do the job given to others. No one ministry can do this alone. We all need each other, and we need all of the people doing the ministries that they have been called to do. The Church will only become the mighty, powerful glorious force on this earth that it was called to be, when each member of the Body is set in place, as God ordained it before the foundation of the earth.

The doctrine of the Nicolaitans (power over the laity; Revelation 2:6; 15), which was already operating in the days of John the Apostle, has become entrenched in the Church of the Lord Jesus Christ. The Lord wants His house to be a training center for His people, where they are perfected, trained and released for the work of the ministry (service). A paradigm shift in our thinking has to take place. Pastors and leaders must transition from: just preaching/teaching to equipping; developing programs to developing leaders; investing in programs to investing in people; focusing only in the needs of their church to focusing in the needs of their community.

The Lord wants His church back, and He is calling all of His people to find their place in ministry. Every believer is called to ministry (to serve), but it is going to take godly leaders, who are not afraid or intimidated by the visions, dreams, anointing and abilities of others, to place each person in their set place, develop the gifting and callings inside of them, teach them how to function and then release them to operate there (Ephesians 4:11-16).

The full revelation of Christ through His body will only come as we begin to function in unity as a body; each believer doing what he has been gifted to do by the Lord. Because God has chosen earthen vessels to manifest His glory and power on the earth, it behooves us to learn and understand Him, His kingdom, His power and His glory, and how He desires to reveal it through us. There are too many people out of place in the Church. People with no anointing, doing things they were never called by God to do, and highly anointed godly vessels sitting in the pews doing nothing. Every ministry and every believer needs to become aligned with God's will for their lives so as to maximize their fruitfulness and usefulness. None of us is worthy to be used of God in this manner, but we understand that it is only by the grace of God that He uses us. Therefore, our focus must always be on Him, and not ourselves.

In the coming years, there will be an unprecedented number of signs and wonders happening all over the world, as the end time harvest of souls is taking place. Maybe you are one of those that God is going to use mightily in the coming years. It is my prayer that this book will help you to understand, discover, and operate in the power of the Holy Spirit, as you grow and develop in the ministry that God intended for you to do on this earth from the foundation of the earth.

1

HINDRANCES TO MOVING IN
IN THE SUPERNATURAL

A. Unbelief

As we begin the study of signs and wonders by the operation of the Holy Spirit, the first thing to put aside is unbelief. Unbelief and skepticism often masquerade as "common sense" and "caution," usually looking upon signs and wonders as being dangerous, causing confusion and disorder. Some even call it "false," "charismatic," "new age" and even "demonic." Although at times in the past, there have been abuses in ministering in the gifts of the Holy Spirit due to flesh, ignorance, lack of proper training on the part of those ministering, and lack of knowledge on the part of the church, those guilty soon found themselves coming up short when God refused to confirm their ministries.

Just because many people have been exposed to something that is false does not mean that the real does not exist. For a false dollar bill to exist there must be a real one. We must leave the comfort zone, and allow the Holy Spirit to lead us into the supernatural realm. There is much to be done, very little time to do it, and very few who believe that God is able to use them in the end time revival and the harvest of souls. Preconceived ideas of how God will or will not work must be put aside as you enter the realm of the supernatural, where His manifest presence is and you allow Him to do His will.

Jesus himself did not do many mighty works in Nazareth because of unbelief (Matthew 13:58; Luke 4:21-29). Unbelief and skepticism will cause God to withhold His miracle working power. He will not manifest His glory in the midst of unbelief (Matthew 17:19-20). If you have been saved, you will speak in new tongues, but that is not all that you should be able to do. (Mark 16:17-18). If you are one of those believers mentioned above, Jesus said that you have the power and authority to cast out devils, heal the sick, and speak in new tongues if you would only believe! One of the things that can stop you is unbelief (Acts 1:8). You must put unbelief and skepticism aside and begin to believe God for the impossible.

As new opportunities present themselves to you or someone else to minister healing to a sick person, do not try to analyze everything and become critical of methods being used, but release your faith and let God do what He wants to do. Do not try to rationalize the moving of the Holy Spirit or explain it away. You will find out that God will do much more for and through those who have child-like, simple faith than those who are always questioning His works and His ways. If God is blessing and using someone in an unusual way and He is being glorified as a result of it, we must learn to bless it too.

B. Fear

Another one of the biggest obstacles in moving with the Holy Spirit is fear of the unknown- of not knowing what to expect next. This shows a lack of trust in God. When we believe in God, love Him, and know that His Word is true and cannot lie, we trust Him and we have no fear. The best antidote for fear is love, and perfect love casts out fear. When we love God with all our hearts, and believe He loves us so much, it has a way of casting out fear from our lives (1 John 4:16-18). We are secure in Him.

People are so afraid that they are going to receive something that is false, that many times they miss out on the real thing. They have been scared into a place where they do not receive any supernatural manifestations of God for fear of accepting something false. The best way to learn how to discern between the true and the false is to get to know the true. If you become familiar with a real dollar bill, you will be able to pick out those false ones instantly. Likewise, if you become intimate with the Lord Jesus Christ, and get to know His Holy Spirit and how He moves and operates, you will be able to discern when someone or something is not of God (Luke 11:9-13; Matthew 7:9-11).

When Jesus came the first time the Jews were so afraid that He was another false prophet that they missed the day of their visitation and the great blessings God had for them. The same things that hindered the Jews from receiving Jesus when He came the first time will hinder us from receiving a visitation from Him and seeing signs and wonders in our midst today.

God desires to manifest His glory on this earth more than we desire it. But most of the time, we do not prepare ourselves or the atmosphere in our services to receive a visitation from the Lord. We can compare it to a large ship coming to dock in our harbor. If we do not make preparations for the arrival of this ship with its precious cargo, the ship will not dock where the harbor is dirty, full of ice and debris but will proceed to dock somewhere else, where they have prepared the harbor for its arrival.

Fear is one of those things that will hinder a move of God in our lives, churches, and cities. For example, there are fears such as the fear of men, fear of the unknown, fear of change, fear of looking silly, fear of losing your reputation or prestige, fear of losing a friend or a position, fear of someone not being healed when you pray for them, fear of giving a word to someone and looking foolish when you miss it, fear of some people looking at you funny, or worse yet laughing at you when you make a fool of yourself in front of everyone. In 1 Corinthians 1:27 the Bible says, *"But God chose the foolish things of the world to confound the wise; God chose the weak things of the world to confound the strong"*. You have to be willing to appear foolish before men to manifest the wisdom and the power of God. Fear of man must be put aside if you are going to be used by God in the gifts of the Holy Spirit. The servant is not above the master. Expect rejection, ridicule, criticism, and persecution when you manifest the power of God on Earth.

C. Pride

Pride or arrogance kills the ministry of the Holy Spirit quicker than any other kind of sin like lying, drinking, or adultery. Pride hides behind various masks and manifests in many different ways, but its root are the same. There is pride of birth, pride of wealth, pride of your reputation, pride of ability, pride of success, pride of personal appearance, pride of self will, pride of temperament, pride of prejudice and pride of pride itself. One time during my travels, I passed a little town that had a welcome sign saying: "We Are Little but Proud".

The pride of your beliefs, doctrine, denomination, and church; the pride of how much you know causing you to despise those that are not one of you, and see them as shallow, inferior, less spiritual or even worse, unsaved; or the pride that makes you think you are the most holy, spiritual, knowledgeable people who are above that kind of emotionalism. It is all called pride and arrogance, and it will kill a move of God's Spirit.

Intelligence is not the key in releasing God's power, or even having great knowledge of the Bible, although we need to know the Word of God and be skillful in using it. The Scribes and Pharisees spent 10-12 hours a day studying the Bible. They studied it all day long, and knew it better than anyone. Yet, when the Messiah came, they knew where He was to be born, but they did not recognize Him. A person may have a great deal of knowledge of the Bible and never hear the voice of God. Jesus told the Scribes and Pharisees that they had never heard the voice of His Father speaking to them (John 5:37). It is the Holy Spirit that gives revelatory knowledge to some people. The Spirit moves through some kinds of people and not others; speaks to some people and not others.

There are some things God is very serious about. When we do those things, it does not matter how smart we are, or how much we know about the Bible. God loves to let His power rest upon the poor, humble and the weak. He resists the proud, but gives grace to the humble (James 4:6 and 1 Peter 5:5). God never commends intelligence or mental ability. He commends wisdom, but is not impressed with human intelligence and does not need it. Proud people have trouble being used by God and hearing His voice because they do not need it. They can figure it out on their own. Knowledge puffs up, but love edifies (1 Corinthians 8:1).

God looks at people differently than we look at people. God's solutions to that person's problems are different from our way of handling problems and applying the solutions.

Our system of theology is not sufficient. If you want the gifts of the Holy Spirit to flow through you, do not put confidence in your own intelligence, in your knowledge of the Bible, in your own ability to hear God, in a denomination, group, etc. The Lord has a way of doing things, and we have another way. The most logical way, frequently, will be the one He does not pick. God is very creative and original, and many times He will ask you to do things which will defy logic and common sense.

Sometimes, He is going to tell you to do something that will make you look foolish. Many times He will insult the mind to reveal the heart. That is why it is so important to be attentive to instructions from the Holy Spirit when ministering to others. Never take the Lord for granted, but always acknowledge Him, and He will direct your paths. When confronted with a difficult situation, ask Him for direction or specific instructions as to how to proceed. The Lord loves when you lean on Him and trust Him.

D. Religious Spirit

The religious spirit is a demon which seeks to substitute religious activity for the power of the Holy Spirit in the believer's life. When Jesus compares the religious spirit to the leaven of the Pharisees, it is because they are very similar in how they work and what they do (Matthew 16:12 and Luke 12:1-2). The leaven in bread does not add substance or nutritional value to the bread, it only inflates it. Likewise, the religious spirit does not add life or any good thing to the church, but it feeds the very pride of man and self-sufficiency. God will not inhabit or use any work that Satan has inflated through pride, and the devil knows that once leaven gets into bread, it is very difficult to remove (2Timothy 3:5; Romans 10:2-11).

Along with pride, the religious spirit is the most difficult stronghold to correct or remove because of its very nature. This spirit deludes people into believing that God is just like them, thus blocking out any rebukes, exhortations, or words of correction, believing that they are for other people and not for them. We won't be able to worship God in spirit and in truth until we free ourselves from this deception. The degree to which we are able to preach the gospel in demonstration and in power is proportional to how much we have been delivered from the powerful and deceptive spirit of religion. A true revelation of God's mercy is the greatest antidote for the religious spirit, and true humility comes as a result of a true revelation of God's mercy and grace.

The religious spirit wants to preserve, at any cost, his way of life or traditions. He feels threatened by anything that comes along that is different from his traditions, and will attack it viciously and without mercy. That is the reason why the Pharisees, who loved the Word of God and their traditions, and hoped for the coming of the Messiah more than anyone else, rejected and persecuted Jesus when He visited them in Israel. They were worshiping traditions more than God. When He did not come having the same regard for their traditions, they rejected Him. These are some warning signs that let us know if a religious spirit is present:

(1) anytime you put more faith in the traditions of men than in the living God (2) When you see as your primary mission the tearing down of what you believe to be wrong, which usually results in a lot of division and not in lasting works that bear fruit (3) a prayer life that is mechanical and done just because you are required to, not desired (4) inability to take rebuke or a word of counsel from others, especially from those you may judge to be less spiritual than yourself (5) the attitude: *"I will not listen to men, only to God"*; and of course, who can argue with what God said (6) seeing what is wrong with others more than what is good in them (7) the belief that you have been appointed to fix everyone and everything (8) when you honor the things that God has done in the past so much that you oppose what He is presently doing (9) being bossy, overbearing, and intolerant of the weaknesses and failures of other people (10) when you compare yourself to others and feel proud that your life or your own ministry is much better, more holy, more spiritual and closer to God than that of others (11) doing things to be seen by others or to be accepted by them (12) a tendency to be suspicious of and oppose anything God is doing, (in reality this is a symptom of jealousy and pride, which are the fruits of the religious spirit), and take a stand that God would not do anything without going through you (13) being overly offended or repulsed by emotional displays in the church or using

emotionalism as a substitute for the work of the Holy Spirit (14) being proud or feeling good when your ministry, church, or spiritual life looks better than others (15) rejecting supernatural manifestations you do not understand, assuming that God's opinions and ways are the same as yours (Isaiah 55:8-12) (16) glorying in anything other than what Jesus Christ did at the Cross of Calvary, and who He is. If we build on anything other than this, we are building on a very shaky foundation that will not stand! The religious spirit will oppose the moving of God's Spirit in power, and will, therefore, be against the manifestation of His gifts in your life and in the church of Jesus Christ (1 Thessalonians 5:19-21).

E.   Spiritual Dullness

The presence of God is very difficult if not impossible to define. However, someone who is sensitive will know when the presence of God is present in a place or when it is absent. The problem is that a lot of Christians live at such a low spiritual level that they are not able to discern the presence or the absence of God in a place. Many have been without the presence of God for so long that it has become the norm, and what is often described as the presence of God, is the misguided opinion of a people out of touch with God.   A church may have lots of activity, enthusiasm, great music, but yet have no awareness of the presence of God.   We have a generation growing up in a religious environment, around religious activities, that have never experienced God's precious presence. The most obvious characteristic of a true revival is an awareness of God. There are some reasons why there is so much spiritual dullness among God's people:

1.   The Holy Spirit has been grieved by sin, pride, strife, legalism, prejudice, unbelief, criticism etc.

2.   Worldliness and carnality. A diet of worldly things will dull your spiritual senses little by little to the point where you will not be able to sense God's presence, and worse yet, not miss Him when He is not there (James 4:4). God will not make an appearance among a people whose priority is not His glory and presence. If you love the world more than the Lord you will forfeit His presence, because you will start to feel self-sufficient and no longer will seek His presence.

3.   Lack of preparation. If you do not pray and spend time with Him, and do not feed on the word of God every day, your spiritual senses will start to become dull.

When people settle for the trappings of religion, and are content to be without the presence of the Lord in their midst, they might as well write ichabod over their life, families and church. They have become no better than the Pharisees of the days of Jesus, who had a form of godliness, but had no presence or power of the Spirit in their midst. Expectancy is replaced by a casual attitude; faith is replaced by unbelief; love is replaced by a cold, critical and unmerciful spirit; and humility is replaced by a proud self-righteous attitude that will make them alienated and insensitive to the Spirit of God.

F.   Prejudice

Throughout the history of mankind, many people have often suffered prejudice at the hands of man. There always seemed to be *"good reasons"* for creating classes in society that would give one group power over another, and keep them marginalized. Prejudice is an offshoot of pride, and often breeds suspicion, intolerance and hatred of other human beings. Although this stronghold still exists today in our society, it should not be a problem with Christians. However, it is shocking to see how many believers and leaders in the church today still seem to have a problem with it.

Prejudice comes in a smattering of shapes and forms, but they are all deadly as they seek to control and manipulate others into submission. Racism is the most common form of prejudice, but not the only one. There are several forms of prejudice still operating in Christianity today, they are:

1.   Racial – how do you overcome racism? Put a g in front of race, and you get grace. God sees the color of the heart, not of the skin. Jesus loves all people alike regardless of race.

2.   Sexual – If woman is the weaker vessel, then that makes man a weak vessel.

3.   Chronological – The very young and old Christians are much neglected in most churches today. That needs to change.

4.   Educational – Jesus died for everyone, regardless of their education or IQ. Paul was educated, Peter was not.

5.   Financial – God does not judge based on pocketbooks.

6.   Physical - Good looks are important to Babylon.

7.   Denominational and Doctrinal – Bickering over non-essentials is still responsible for separating the body of Christ.

G.   Lack of Love

We read in the Bible that Jesus was full of grace and truth. He came to this earth to reveal to us the heart of the Father. It is God's nature to love and to be loved. As a matter of fact, the Bible says that God is love; and everyone that practices love is born of God and knows God. He that does not love does not know God, for God is love (1 John 4:7-8). If we are to taste and partake of the presence and the glory of God to be revealed in these last days, we must rid ourselves of any hardness of heart, and indifference towards the suffering and hurts of others and clothe ourselves with love and compassion.

Compassion is love in action. Lack of love or compassion will hinder you from seeing the glory of God. The Lord does not like to manifest His presence and power in the midst of a people of hard and cold hearts. The Holy Spirit is grieved when surrounded by these negative emotions of prejudice, hatred, strife, criticism, un-forgiveness, bitterness and lack of love.   All these traits manifest a lack of mercy and grace, and total misunderstanding of what love really is.

God will not rest His anointing and power on people that do not reflect His love. As a matter of fact, all of the gifts of the Holy Spirit flow on the basis of love and compassion. God has mercy on His people.   The Bible says that Jesus was moved with compassion (Mathew 9:36). Today, the Lord is still moved with compassion in the person of the Holy Spirit within us.   It takes humility to be able to refrain from judging and criticizing others, and instead to identify with them in their situation.

The proverbial Indian saying, "do not criticize your neighbor until you have walked twenty miles in his moccasins" holds true. When the Samaritans did not receive Jesus because He was on His way to Jerusalem, James and John were ready to call fire from heaven and destroy them (Luke 9:54-56). Jesus rebuked them harshly for their lack of love and compassion for these people. Many times we are guilty of the same thing.

The same is true in the story of Jonah. Here was a prophet who God used to warn Nineveh of impending judgment. At first however, Johan disobeyed God and wound up in the belly of the big fish. When he finally decided to obey God, reluctantly he preached repentance to Nineveh. But to his surprise, the city of Nineveh, from the king all the way down to the animals, fasted and repented in sackcloth, and turned from their evil ways (Jonah 3:6-10; 2 Chronicles 7:14). This held back the judgment of God upon Nineveh. However, Jonah became very angry at God for not destroying Nineveh. The Lord rebuked him for not having compassion on the inhabitants of Nineveh. Although Johan was a man of God, he did not show love or compassion for the people of that city.

Likewise there are many today who have the spirit of Jonah. They are quick to judge and condemn, but show no mercy or compassion for the people. Nineveh deserved to be destroyed, but God is not willing that any should perish, but that all men proceed to repentance. Instead of condemning people, cities or nations, we need to pray for them. Sometimes when people go through a lot of pain and torment inflicted by others, they build walls around them to protect themselves. The problem is that by building walls, they cut off the Lord as well and their hearts become hard and insensitive.

Those who want to be in ministry (service) need to learn to love people, even the unlovable ones. You can bring prophetic words all you want, but if those words are not backed with the love of God, your words will be hollow and dry like sounding brass or clanging cymbal (1 Corinthians 13:1). If you have noticed that the gifts are not flowing through the way they should or they stopped flowing through you, chances are that you have neglected the love of God in your life. You see, if you do not have love working together with faith, you will only go so far and no further.

It is easy to be mean and hard, and hate others when they do you wrong. But no one can react against love. Love can get into places of the human heart that nothing else can. When you come to a place where you understand that you were created for love and to love God above all things, and your neighbor as yourself, you will have begun your long journey into understanding the heart of God. Love is the language of heaven.

God wants to manifest the nature of His Son in our lives. As we spend time with Him and we behold Him, we will receive His Divine impartation and we will be transformed from glory to glory as we are transformed into His image. If we want to bring heaven down to earth, we better prepare ourselves to walk in a spirit of love and humility.

2

UNDERSTANDING THE UNITY OF THE VISIBLE AND INVISIBLE REALMS

A. Understanding the Spiritual Realm

There was an article that appeared recently on Time Magazine that talked about how scientists have discovered that we live in multi-dimension or multilayered world similar to an onion. This is something that the Bible has always stated by referring to several heavens. There are two realms existing side-by-side. One is the natural and visible realm, which is discerned by our five senses, and the other is the spiritual and invisible realm, which is discerned spiritually.

Man was created in the image of God. As God is a tripartite being, so is man: Father, Son and Holy Spirit – Soul (psyche, mind, will and emotions), body (bios, outer shell), and spirit (ZOË, heart, innermost being). Before a person is born again, the spirit of man is so submerged by the soul that he could not tell the difference between the two. Because man's spirit lost communion with God, its function became so eclipsed and governed by the soul that it was ignored. That is why when a person is born again, it becomes necessary to separate the spirit from the soul.

In the Bible, the tabernacle blueprint given to us also is divided into three parts. Your have the outer court, the holy place and the holy of holies. The analogy here to us is as follows: body (outer court), soul (holy place) and the spirit (holy of holies). All three parts are interconnected.

The body is the part of us that makes us conscious of the world, and helps us stay in touch with the world through the five senses. These are the only signals our mind can understand and process. Apparently, there is a spiritual counterpart to each of the five natural senses. (Colossians

1:16; 2 Corinthians 4:8). When Jesus said, *"HE THAT HAS AN EAR, LET HIM HEAR"* (Revelation 2:7), it is clear that He was not speaking about the natural ear. We all have natural ears, but not all have spiritual ears. (Hebrews 5:14). This scripture is not referring to the natural senses, but to the spiritual senses.

The soul is much more than just our intellectual mind as it is the point of contact between the spirit and body. The soul is between the world of the spirit and the body, and belongs to both, keeping the spirit and body united. It is tied to the world through our spirit, and to the material world through our bodies. The soul is the seat of our emotions, will and personality and it represents the real you. You may have heard before that we are a spirit, have a soul and live in a body. In the beginning, our spirits governed our minds, and our minds told our bodies what to do. After the fall, the whole thing was reversed and we are governed by our bodies, telling our minds what to do. When we are born again, the process is again reversed where our spirits once again (should) rule our lives.

Our spirit is the part that helps us sense God and the spiritual realm. It is the noblest part of us, and occupies the deepest part of our being. It helps us to communicate with God and allows us to worship God. God lives in the spirits of born-again believers. Just like the body is the covering for the soul, the soul is the covering for the body. The spirit cannot act directly on the body, it needs the soul.

The natural senses are simply transmitters of information, and are not able to discern between good and evil. The scripture, *"O TASTE AND SEE THAT THE LORD IS GOOD"* (Psalm 34:8) is not an invitation to use our natural taste buds, but is a reference to a spiritual sense of taste. Jesus talked of an *"evil eye"* in Matthew 6:23. But here, once again, He is not referring to the physical eye which only transmits information. Behind it, and beneath it, is a spiritual eye which is used in looking unto Jesus (Hebrews 9:24). There is a spiritual sense of smell (Amos 5:21 and Philippians 4:18), and there is a spiritual sense of feeling, indicated in Ephesians 4:19.

In the beginning, God's intention was that there would be no division between the visible and the invisible realms, but that there would be a perfect union between the two.

26

The visible realm was to reflect the spiritual or invisible realm (Hebrew 8:5; 9:24). Because of this perfect union which existed between the realms in the Garden of Eden, Adam and Eve could hear the voice of God (Genesis 3:8). Our spirit man was in total control of our soul (mind, emotions, will etc.), and our soul was in control of our body. When Adam and Eve sinned, the spirit of man lost its ability to see and hear the spirit realm.

Sin drove a wedge between God and man, separating the physical and the spiritual realms. Jesus came as the second Adam to restore the relationship between man and God, the visible and invisible realms that the first Adam lost through disobedience, so that man could once again hear God and be able to partake of the invisible realm through the blood of Jesus (Hebrews 10:19-20).

Success in flowing in the supernatural will come when we are sensitive enough to the Holy Spirit to bring over into the natural realm, those things available in the spiritual realm. The key to the success of the earthly ministry of Jesus was that He attempted nothing by the power of the flesh. He was so spiritually sensitive that He looked over into the realm of the Spirit, and did only what He saw His Father doing. (John 5:17-20, 30, and 36).

The unity between the visible and the invisible worlds found perfect expression in the ministry of Jesus. He only did what He saw His Father doing with the eye of the spirit. This harmony was so intimate and perfect that Jesus could truthfully say that the Father showed Him all things that He did. Jesus acted out in the natural, visible realm the works which He saw happen in the spiritual world. He did, in the physical realm, what God was doing in the spiritual realm.

Since Jesus moved in perfect harmony with the Spirit, His ministry never failed. When He said to the man in Bethesda, *"Take-up your bed and walk"* (John 5:8), He was not merely praying and hoping that it would be God's will to heal that man, at that time. Instead, He saw that it was the kairos time to heal the man's infirmity, and merely acted on what He saw happening in the spirit realm. This explains why none of the other cripples there were healed (John 5:2-3). In the sovereign timing of God, it was time for only one of them to be healed.

Some people, who do not believe in laying hands on the

sick, have in the past said sarcastic things like, "Why don't you go to hospitals and empty them out?" The pool of Bethesda was a sort of hospital of its time. There were many sick people there all the time, but Jesus healed only one. We may not understand why it was not God's time to heal any of the others, but we can't question God.

Success in ministering spiritual gifts comes when we are so perfectly in tune with what God is doing in the spiritual realm, that we only do those things we see happening in the spirit realm. Any time you go beyond that and start doing something in the flesh, it will always result in failure.

B.   People Who Saw Into the Spiritual Realm

Throughout the Old and the New Testaments, there were many people who saw into the spirit realm and received revelation, deliverance, and instruction. In the book of Hebrews 11:27 we read that Moses saw the invisible God. Joshua saw an angel that was the captain of the Lord's hosts, who gave him instructions on how to take over the city of Jericho (Joshua 5:13-15).

Elisha prayed that his servant could see the chariots of fire who were around them to protect them (II Kings 6:15-18). John the Baptist saw the Spirit of God descending from heaven upon Jesus in the form of a dove (John 1:32).

The early church began with a visible glimpse into the realm of the Spirit, when cloven tongues as of fire, were seen resting upon each one of the believers in the upper room (Acts 2:3, 17). Stephen saw a vision of the Lord in Heaven (Acts 7:55-56). On two occasions, an angel of the Lord came to get Peter out of prison (Acts 5:19; 12:7-11). Peter also saw a vision from Heaven regarding the preaching of the Gospel to the Gentiles, and even argued with the Lord about it (Acts 10:10-16).

Cornelius, the Italian centurion, saw a vision of an angel giving him a message from God (Acts 10:3-4). Saul of Tarsus had a vision of Jesus, Himself, on his journey to Damascus (Acts 9:3-6). The Lord spoke to Ananias in a vision, giving him instructions and specific information (Acts 9:10-11). The great apostle Paul had several experiences recorded in the Bible (Acts 18:9-10; 27:22-24 and II

Corinthians 12:2-4). Last, but not least, is the beloved apostle John, who received a number of apocalyptic visions recorded in the Book of Revelation.

There are many other examples we could mention, of Christian men and women who saw into the spiritual realm and were mightily used of God to advance His Kingdom on this earth. Most of them lived during the 20th century; many others lived in the preceding centuries, after the apostolic age came to an end with the death of the apostle John in 96 A.D. They are a testimony to the truth contained in the words of Jesus when He said...

C.   Greater Works Than These Shall You Do

In the book of John 14:10-14, Jesus said that we would do the same works He did when He was on the earth, and not only the same works, but greater works would we do because He was going to the Father. Just as the success of the ministry of Jesus was due to the fact that He attempted to do nothing in the flesh, but relied totally on what He saw occurring in the spirit realm, so likewise, our success will be based upon whether we become sensitive to the Spirit, and only do what He is showing us rather than trying to do things in the flesh or on whims.

Jesus said that those who believed on Him would do greater works. What does the record say about the early Christians? Please read the following scriptures: (Acts 2:43; 3:1-8; 5:12-16; 6:8; 8:7,13,39-40; 9:10, 32-42; 11:27-28; 13:9-12; 14:3, 8-10; 16:9-10,14-18, 25-34; 18:9-10; 19:11-12; 20:9-12; 23:11; 27:21-26; 28:1-10).

It seems that, just as Jesus said, even greater works were done by His followers after His ascension than He did while He was on the earth. Of course, it was not really the believers doing the works, but it was the Lord doing the works through them, just as the Father had done mighty works through Jesus when He was on the earth. This helps us to understand the significance of John 14:13-14 a little more clearly.

This does not refer to an indiscriminate use of His name as a kind of a magic talisman, where we just tack on the words *"in Jesus name"* onto our request. But it means asking by His authority, in the same sense that

29

Jesus came in His Father's name (John 5:36). In other words, we ask in His name when we *"know"* that it is His will to bring something to pass, and therefore have the permission and authority of heaven to do something, or say something. (John 5:17; 14:17-21, 26; 15:7, 15-16; 14:12-14 and I John 5:14-15).

But how do we know the will of God? We know the general will from His written Word, the Bible. But how do we know His specific will? How do we see over into the realm of the spirit know what He is doing? Through the gifts of the Spirit, we are able to see over into the spirit realm, or hear and feel intuitively spiritual things.

Through the word of wisdom, we receive direction and revelation concerning the future. Through the word of knowledge, we receive factual information from either the past or the present of any particular person or case. Through the discerning of spirits, we are able to see what spirit is at work in a given situation.

Through the working of miracles, signs and wonders we go beyond natural laws, and are able perform supernatural acts that do not normally happen. Through the gifts of healings, we are able to reverse the process of sickness in a person's body. Through the gift of faith, we are able to see the impossible as being possible, and make prophetic decrees. Through diverse kinds of tongues, interpretation of tongues, and prophecy we speak in God's stead for edification, exhortation and comfort of the body of Christ.

Please bear in mind that all the gifts of the Spirit always come in clusters. When one is manifesting, there will always be others present. That is the beauty and the genius of the Holy Spirit in manifesting various gifts through different people towards the same goal. No one person is ever going to have every gift of the Spirit flowing through them at the same time. That is why God made each of us different, so we would need each other.

This helps us to understand Mark 16:17-20. When believers enter into this type of ministry, and are trained to operate in the supernatural realm, it will be like the ministry of Jesus multiplied over hundreds of thousands of times, having a staggering impact on the world.

3

THE NINE GIFTS OF
THE HOLY SPIRIT

A. How the Gifts Work Together

In 1 Corinthians 12:8-10, we find a description of the nine gifts of the Holy Spirit. The spiritual gifts are usually divided into three groups:

The Revelation Gifts
The Word of Wisdom
The Word of Knowledge
The Discerning of Spirits

The Power Gifts
The Gift of Faith
Gifts of Healings
The Working of Miracles

The Vocal Gifts
The Gift of Tongues
Gifts of Interpretation
The Gift of Prophecy

It is important to mention that these groupings are only for the sake of identification. The person who begins to operate in the gifts of the Spirit will soon discover that, in reality, several of the gifts will work together to accomplish a common goal. For example, a person operating in the gifts of healings may find out that the word of knowledge is working in conjunction with that gift, giving him information about the sick person's condition. Then the word of wisdom may come to give direction to that individual. The gifts of the Spirit are given to believers who

31

are members of a mystical body, to give them their specific function in the body. Likewise, it is seen that all the gifts operate together, complementing each other to achieve the desired result.

It would be silly if the arm, the leg, the eye, the ear, and the mouth would be identified, severed from each other, and without body cooperation among them. Therefore, the spiritual must operate in harmony, just as the members of the human body operate to help each other. We must learn that there is power in unity as we work together, using our gifts and callings to the mutual benefit, and for the benefit of the body.

B. The Word of Wisdom

The thing to notice here is the gift of the *"word"* of wisdom. It is not the gift of wisdom. This is not to be confused with the Godly wisdom which we are encouraged to seek (Proverbs 3:13-20; 4:5-13; James 1:5). The gift of the word of wisdom is a *"small portion of God's total wisdom that is supernaturally imparted by the Holy Spirit"*. It is also very important not to confuse wisdom with knowledge. Knowledge is information, while wisdom is the ability to know what to do with that information and be able to apply it correctly (Ecclesiastes 10:10). If the axe is blunt, the workman may still be able to chop down the tree, but he will take more time, strength, and effort. If the axe is sharp, the task will be completed much more quickly, easily, and cleanly.

Likewise, we may be able to accomplish a spiritual task without wisdom, but it will require more effort and take longer. The word of wisdom will help get the job done more quickly, smoothly, with a minimum of flesh and with the least amount of damage. Wisdom and knowledge work together. Knowledge must be directed by wisdom, or it will be used unwisely (Proverbs 15:2). Some examples of the word of wisdom in operation are found in Luke 5:4-10; Matthew 21:1-7; Acts 6:1-7; 8:26-29; 10:9-16; 15:13-29; 16:6-10. Many times when the Lord reveals something to me and tells me to do something which may not make much sense, He is in fact giving me a word of wisdom.

I have witnessed the word of wisdom produce great conviction in the lives of people, open their hearts to receive the gospel, and open the door in a church service to minister to many people. It is a supernatural revelation, by the Holy Spirit, of divine purposes. It is a supernatural declaration of the mind and will of God about His plans and purposes concerning things, places and people. In this sense, the word of wisdom often operates through the spoken word, thus having some similarity to the word of knowledge, prophecy, and the interpretation of tongues.

How will you know if the word of wisdom is moving in you? Most people who operate in this gift report that the vocal gifts originate as an impression, a thought, or a word which pops-up, unbidden, into their minds. Most people do not receive the complete message in advance, but as they speak what they have, the Holy Spirit supplies more of the message until it is complete. Some report seeing the words on a scroll, or a screen, or a visual picture, which they must then learn to interpret correctly.

This is where many, who may have genuinely received a word or a vision from the Lord, make a mistake. They try to interpret it, and many times do so incorrectly, thus bringing confusion and reproach upon the ministry of the gifts of the Spirit. Most of the time, if I do not receive a clear interpretation of what I have seen in the spirit realm, I just share what I saw with the person I am ministering to, and ask him if it means anything to them. In my experience, things which make absolutely no sense to me are highly significant to people. It may be a flower, a broken toy, a boat, or another picture that symbolically represents an important event in the life of the individual. Share it with simplicity and faith, and watch the Holy Spirit do His work. After all, He knows what to do better than anyone else, and will work with us if we give Him the opportunity.

C. The Word of Knowledge

This gift is not to be confused with knowledge about scriptures, or other things in the natural. The word of knowledge is information concerning something about which the person has absolutely no personal knowledge, and is revealed to him by the Spirit. It is not suspicion or guesswork. Some examples of the word of knowledge are found in John 1:47-49, 4:16-19, Acts 5:1-11, 9:11-12, 10:19-23, and 21:10-11. The word of knowledge produces conviction, confirmation and also preparation. It may come in the form of a name, place, disease, or other piece of information in the life of someone to which you have no access.

As in the word of wisdom, the word of knowledge comes unbidden into the mind, or comes as an impression, thought, word, or picture. In the case of the operation of the gifts of healings, a person may feel the other's pain in his own body, or he may see the affected part of the body in some way, so as to understand it needs healing.

Often, the word of knowledge will be followed by other gifts, such as the gifts of healings, the working of miracles, the gift of faith, the word of wisdom, or prophecy. It opens the door, many times, to minister to the person effectively. I have seen how a word of knowledge often has opened up a person, or even the service in a church, to the ministry of the Holy Spirit. It frequently brings the fear of the Lord and reverence, which in turn, changes the atmosphere in the service and makes it conducive for signs and wonders to take place.

I have seen big, tough men cry like children and repent before God after the manifestation of a word of knowledge. On the other hand, I have also seen a word of knowledge produce great inner healing, joy, and laughter in others. We must always remember that the Holy Spirit deals with two people in entirely different manners. One thing is for sure, God will never force any person to operate in the gifts of the Spirit.

If you are waiting on God to force you to operate in a particular gift, you will never be used in this ministry. At some point, you are going to have to exercise your faith, for faith without works is dead. You must take what the Holy Spirit has given you, and give expression to it. Many people have this gift inside of them, but have never activated it. Ask the Holy Spirit to teach you how to use His gifts. He is our best teacher.

D. The Discerning of Spirits

Sometimes, this gift is confused with the word of knowledge, or called the gift of discernment. The word *"discern"* means to recognize and distinguish between. The one operating in this gift will recognize what spirits are at work in a given situation. It is important to know that there are several kinds of spirits: (a) the Holy Spirit (b) angels of God (c) fallen angels (d) demons or evil spirits (e) human spirits. Some examples of the discerning of spirits are found in John 1:32-33, 47, 20:23-24, Luke 13:11-17, 22:43, Matthew 9:32-34,12:22-24, Mark 9:17-27, Acts 2:3, 8:20-24, 14:8-10, 16:16-18, and 27:23-24.

Those who are used in this gift report seeing a vision where spirits are seen in the form of animals. For example, the Holy Spirit was seen in the form of a dove, and unclean spirits as frogs (John 1:32 and Revelation 16:13). Sometimes, the discernment takes the form of seeing people as they are spiritually: crooked, unclean, and/or with satanic features. However, this gift operates more commonly in the form of a spiritual interpretation of what the natural senses show. Many have reported seeing angels.

I remember several years ago, we were ministering in Nashville, Tennessee, and there was an unusual moving of the Holy Spirit in the morning service. Many people were being healed and delivered from demonic oppressions while we were ministering. After the service, we were invited to have lunch with the pastor and his wife at the home of one of the members of the church. While we were there, the sister who invited us told us how, while I was ministering to the people, she saw this huge angel standing behind me, with a golden girdle on, and a hand on his sword.

But, while many are used in this gift by seeing the spirit world, others do not see, they simply know what spirit is at work. They know when there is an angel in the room, or a demon, or what spirit is working in the life of a person who needs deliverance. It is important to keep in mind that the main reason the Holy Spirit gives us information supernaturally, is so that we are able to do something about it.

As we step out in faith with the information we have received, He will continue to supply additional information or direction until we have accomplished His purpose in that particular situation.

E. The Gift of Faith

It is important to understand, that there are three different types of faith referred to in the New Testament: (1) the faith that comes by hearing the word of God (Romans 10:17) (2) the faith that is a part of the fruit of the Spirit (Galatians 5:22) (3) the gift of faith given by the Holy Spirit (I Corinthians 12:9). There is, of course, a great difference between the fruit and the gift of faith.

Fruit is a natural outgrowth due to the nature of the tree. It must be cultivated with care and labor (II Timothy 2:6). A gift, on the other hand, is something that grows over a period of time, but that is freely given. Fruit reveals something about a person's character, whereas a gift says nothing about the character of the person. The faith that is a fruit of the Spirit is best described as a quiet trust in the Lord.

The gift of faith can be operated in two different ways: (1) you can speak words to God on behalf of a person, object or situation (I Kings 17:1; 18:41-45; James 5:16-18). (2) You can speak words to a person, object or situation on God's behalf (Joshua 10: 12-14; Mark 4:39-41; 11:12-14, 20-24; Matthew 17:20; Luke 7:12-15; 8:54-55; John 11:43-44; Acts 9:40; 13:9-12; 16:16-18; I Corinthians 13:2). This gift, when in operation, causes a dramatic assurance to come upon the person, to accomplish something miraculous. There is no doubt, only confidence and conviction. You may also even experience a sensation of well-being, joyous abandon and holy boldness. This gift often operates by using short commands: *"RISE!"*, *"BE HEALED IN THE NAME OF JESUS!"*, *"LAZARUS, COME FORTH!"* OR *"RISE UP AND WALK!*

I remember an incident several years ago, when I saw this gift operate through me. Before I became a preacher, I used to work in an engineering firm, where I had a parking space assigned to me. I was happy with my parking space, except that it had a tree next to it which produced these obnoxious black berries that kept falling on top of my brand new car and ruining the enamel. I tried to have my parking space changed, but to no avail. One day, as I was leaving, I came to my car and found it covered with berries. I felt righteous indignation rise up within me, and before I could think twice I said in a loud voice, *"I CURSE YOU AT THE ROOT AND COMMAND YOU TO DRY UP AND DIE!"* I got into my car, and without giving it any further thought, I went home. The next day when I got to work, to my surprise I found all the berries and the leaves on the ground, and the branches in the tree dry and without leaves.

F. The Gifts of Healings

A healing occurs gradually, sometimes overnight or over a period of days, relieving the body of pain and disease. A miracle is instantaneous, usually perceptible to the eye, going beyond healing. For example, a leg may be lengthened, a missing eyeball created, or internal organs replaced, even when they have previously been surgically removed. It is interesting to notice, that this gift is called *"The Gifts of Healings,"* and not *"The Gift of Healing."* The reason for this is that there may be different gifts for various diseases. Some seem to be gifted to heal certain, specific problems. For example: deafness, blindness, back problems, cancer, tumors, etc. A person with a gift in one area may operate in some other areas, but with a much lower success rate. This gift usually works through physical contact. Examples: Mark 5:30, 7:32-35, 8:22-26, Luke 4:40, 6:19, Acts 5:15 and 28:8. Each person may discover that a certain method works best for him in ministering healing Following are some insights for operating in these gifts:

1. Try to lay hands specifically on the area of the body affected by the disease. If the person receiving ministry is of a different sex than you, you need to exercise wisdom. You may ask the sick person to lay his/her hand on the affected part as you pray or you may ask another person of the same sex to place her hand over the sick part of the body. Jesus always touched the specific body part. Remember that obedience is extremely important as the Holy Spirit may ask you to do something different and

creative that no one has done before.

2. Minister with your eyes open. Nothing in the scriptures tell us to minister with our eyes open, but it does not tell us to close them, either. If you close your eyes, you will miss seeing what the Spirit is doing on the person. Do not call this ministry *"praying for the sick,"* but *"ministering healing."* In the New Testament, we don't see Jesus or His disciples praying for the sick, they healed the sick. (Matthew 10:8; Acts 3:6, 9:40, 13:11, 14:10, 20:10, 28:8). The One who heals is living within us. Command that sickness to go, and healing to come. The more specific you pray, the better the result. Speak to the afflicted part of the body and command it to be made whole. Ask the person where the pain is and what the problem is. Jesus sometimes interviewed those that came to Him for healing.

3. It is often helpful to move the afflicted part of the body after healing is ministered to a person. Jesus commanded the man with the withered arm to stretch it forth. He commanded the blind man to wash in the pool of Siloam. Peter took the lame man by the hand and lifted him up. This releases faith in the person, and often, it is at that precise moment that healing takes place. Once again, let the Holy Spirit guide you as to how He wants to heal the person.

4. After you minister healing, ask the person if the pain is gone. If they are hurting, you can tell instantly if they were healed. If, after you minister healing, they still feel some discomfort, do it again. Remember, even Jesus ministered to a blind man twice. Some need to be prayed over two, three, or more times before they are healed. Many times, God is removing obstacles and healing areas that are hindering them from receiving physical healing. We have a spirit man inside of us, and often, he has to be healed before our body is.

G. The Working of Miracles

While it has some similarities with healings, miracles go beyond them. Miracles are something supernatural, instantaneous and may not involve the body of a person at all. They may involve an object like the tree Jesus cursed, or the multiplication of bread, or the turning of water into wine. Miracles are contrary to nature. They involve the impossible. Casting out devils falls in the realm of the miraculous (Mark 9:38-39, Acts 8:7, 13). Miracles took place when pieces of cloth anointed by Paul were placed on people who were sick, and they were healed, and evil spirits left (Acts 19:11-12, John 2:6-11, and 6:8-14). While the gifts of healings may heal a person slowly, and still accomplish the same purpose, a miracle will happen suddenly, and will instantly deliver someone from an affliction, pain, tumor, cancer or even go into the creative area, where parts of the human body are recreated to replace damaged ones or even missing ones.

I have seen cases where tumors, goiters and hernias have instantly disappeared in people, as they were commanded to go in the name of Jesus. These things fall under the category of miracles. When signs and wonders start happening in a service, it brings the level of faith of the congregation up higher to a place where anything can happen.

There is one incident that took place in Miami, Florida. A lady was suffering from a condition in her lungs; she had a hole in one of the lungs which was infected and was causing her great pain and distress. The doctors had given her no hope of ever getting better. When she came up for prayer, the power of God came upon her and she was slain in the spirit. After she came to herself, she felt her lungs burning, and all the pain was gone from her. Some time later, she went to the doctor, and after they took an X-ray, discovered that the hole in her lung was gone. When the doctors checked her, they could not believe it.

Another incident took place several years ago, while my wife and I were on our way to church. Suddenly, our car's motor turned off for no reason as we came to a stop light, right by a gas station. As we waited for our car to be fixed, a little dog was run over and killed by an automobile, right in front of us. We were so affected by this incident that we ran over to where the dog was lying. He was dead alright. Without giving it another thought, we prayed for the dog to come back to life. To our astonishment, he suddenly opened his eyes, jumped to his feet, and ran away. This was our first miracle of resurrection. We didn't go to church that night, but we had church right there in the street, as we experienced the miracle-working power of God.

Casting devils out of people is something that is not practiced much in Christianity today, especially in this nation, yet one third of the ministry of Jesus consisted in casting demons out of people. Through the years, we have seen many demonized delivered and set free. The spirits came out screaming in agony, launching threats, and saying unclean words. Most of the time as they come out, they produce retching and vomiting in the people. During the seven years we pastored in Miami, Florida, we saw many people that came out of the occult, Santeria, witchcraft and Satanism. Many of these people needed heavy personal ministry even after they were converted and baptized in water.

There was one particular case that comes to my mind. One day, a small, middle-aged man brought his mother to our church for service. During that service, the power of God came upon him, and he was thrown down to the floor, shaking and convulsing. We took him to a little room in the back of the church, which we had nicknamed *"the clinic."* While we were ministering to him, we found out that he used to be a very famous spiritist in Cuba. People would wait outside his home to be first in line to see him the next day. He used to be called *"the prodigy child of Guanabo,"* because of his ability to tell people what was going on in their lives and foretell their future. That day we cast four spirits that manifested through him, and he has been free ever since.

H. The Gift of Prophecy

It should be noted that there is a difference between the ministry of the prophet, and a person having the gift of prophecy. Although all prophets have the gift of prophecy operating in them, not everyone who has the gift of prophecy is a prophet. The office of a prophet is an ascension gift to the church (Ephesians 4:11) and one of the five-fold ministries. A prophet is a spokesman for God; an oracle of God who is used to reveal some truth, warn of some impending danger, or prepare a people for some future event coming upon them (Ephesians 3:5, 4:11-16, Acts 13:1, 1 Corinthians 12:28-29).

In the case of a prophet, the person himself is a gift to the church, including every aspect of his ministry and character that makes up the gift. In the case of the person that is not a prophet but has the gift of prophecy, the gift is given to and through the believer, but the believer himself is not the gift. The gift of prophecy is a brief, spiritual manifestation rather than a ministry office involving every aspect of the person's life. Character is not involved, it is a gift. Prophecy is an act of prophesying, while a prophet is an office that a person was called to and walks in after years of preparation and process (I Corinthians 14:25-33). When prophecy comes through a prophet, the message or words have more anointing, weight and authority than the gift of prophecy that flows through a Christian believer.

Like all the gifts of the Spirit, the gift of prophecy is subject to the control of the person. Paul gets into the regulations for proper use of this gift in 1 Corinthians 14:1-33. This gift, along with the gifts of tongues and interpretations, is one of the most common gifts found in the church and the most desirable of the vocal gifts, according to the teaching of Paul in 1 Corinthians 14:1-3.

The gift of prophecy must fulfill the following three requirements:

1.   *Edification* - This means that the word of prophecy must build up and bring strength to those that are receiving it.

2.   Exhortation - This has to do with a prophetic word providing encouragement to those that hear it.

3.   Comfort - This tells us that the prophetic word must bring hope, healing to the afflicted, consolation, and joy to those troubled and sad. If the prophetic word does not fulfill the above mentioned requirements, it is not to be received as from God.

Genuine prophecy will never bring condemnation, discouragement, seek to praise man or establish a doctrine or belief that someone has shared. It is often used to confirm a ministry to which a person is called, confirm a person in a particular ministry, or confirm a message that is shared in a service (Read 1 Timothy

41

1:18, 4:14). Prophecy is to be given according to one's faith (Romans 12:6).

There will, at times, be the temptation to go beyond one's faith and fall into the realm of the carnal prophecy. Prophecy will never force or compel a person to speak or say anything apart from his own will (1 Corinthians 14:29-33). This is the main difference between the Holy Spirit and an evil spirit, which will compel a person to act in certain ways and say certain things. All prophecy must align itself with the Word of God. The Bible is the railroad upon which all supernatural manifestations of God's Spirit must travel. Genuine prophecy will always glorify God, and produce fruit in the person receiving it that is in agreement with Romans 14:17, Galatians 5:22-23, and Matthew 7:15-16.

False prophecy is also identified by its fruit, which is: exaggeration, arrogance, boastfulness, lust, pride, dishonesty, greed, financial irresponsibility, immorality, licentiousness, broken homes, etc. (Matthew 7:21-22, 2 Peter 2:15-16). Genuine prophecy will produce liberty, love, peace, and life. It will not produce fear, bondage, confusion, or death (2 Corinthians 3:17, Romans 8:15; 1 Corinthians 14:33, and II Timothy 1:7).

True prophecy will always bring a refreshing presence of God into the services, and will harmonize with the Scriptures (I2 Corinthians 3:6). A true, genuine prophecy will always bear witness by the Holy Spirit within each believer who hears it (1 John 2:27 and Romans 8:16). The prophetic word will often come upon the believer in very much the same way as the word of knowledge or wisdom, whereby he receives an impression, thought, or words into his mind which did not originate with him.

Also, the person may see the words or have a mental picture which he will describe. Some receive the entire prophecy in advance. However, most of the time, it is received only in parts, usually the leading part of the prophecy. Then, as the believer steps out in faith to speak that which he has received, more of the message comes to him until it is completed.

It is not unusual for those upon whom the Spirit of prophecy comes, to experience physical sensations of unusual quality. These may include a rapid heartbeat, a sense of excitement, a feeling that one will burst out if he does not speak, or some other sensation out of the ordinary. However, the person giving the prophecy will be able to hold on to the prophetic word until an opening in the service is provided so he can share the prophecy.

A person who has this gift operating in his life will usually only be given a phrase, and he will launch out in faith. Another may hear or see them on a screen. Another may have a general thought which he puts into words of his own choosing. Still another may see a vision or mental picture and relate what he sees.

When you are used in this gift take care to speak plainly and slowly that even a child can understand, and loud enough for all to hear. Take your time. If this is in a large auditorium, you should try to obtain a microphone over which to give the interpretation. Speak with confidence, zeal and anointing knowing that God is speaking through you when God releases you to speak, but when the Holy Spirit ceases to lead, stop speaking or you will quickly get into a carnal area by adding to the word the Holy Spirit has already given.

In 1 Corinthians 14:32-33, the apostle Paul states that the spirits of the prophets are subject to the prophets. In other words, people have the ability to hold or control the outflow of the gift until the proper time has come to share it in the service. God is not the Author of confusion and will not interrupt the preaching of the Word to give a prophecy.

If you fumble or make mistakes do not stop, but keep on going and the Holy Spirit will help you. Do not slouch or stand in a casual way, but stand up with dignity and boldness. Never be afraid to share what the Holy Spirit has given you, even if it is only a few words or just a simple picture. Share what He has given you with humility and in obedience and He will give you more.

It is important that you do not speak and share if the Lord has not spoken to you or is not flowing through you. People sometimes become so desperate to speak forth a word from the Lord that they get into the flesh. Remain calm and wait for the Lord to speak. Do not dominate a meeting by doing all the sharing. You must learn to step back and give a chance to some of the others to speak and share what the Lord has given them.

Never share people's sins or private things in public. The Lord is a gentleman and never embarrasses people. Never deliver a word in anger or to prove a point. You will only cause strife, doubt, confusion, bitterness and hurt feelings. If you must err, it is better to err on the side of love, grace and compassion. Remember Jesus moved with compassion (Matthew 9:36, 14:14; Mark 1:41, 6:34).

Submit to the authority over you in the house. Do not impose your ministry on others; no one will receive it if you force yourself on them. Wait for the right time and moment; if the Lord is in it, He will make a way. If the prophetic words the Lord has given you disagree with the leadership of the house, first share the word with them. If they decide not to receive it, you have done your part and operated in order and they will be held accountable by the Lord. The only time when a prophetic decree can be given in authority is if you stand in prophetic office.

Like all vocal gifts of the Spirit, it would be wise to record them on a cassette tape to be played later for future reference to judge and to learn by past mistakes. Like all the gifts of the Spirit, when this gift first starts manifesting in a person's life, it will come out imperfect, rough, and may not flow as we would like it. Pray that God will send you a man of God who is flowing in the gifts of the Spirit and has the heart of a father, who will mentor you and train you to move in the supernatural.

The key to be successful is to keep doing it, not to stop just because you do not succeed at first. You will learn by doing and making mistakes. Bear in mind that growing and maturing in the gifts of the Spirit, as in anything else, is a process that takes time, patience and practice. While we are in these bodies of clay, we will make mistakes, but the Lord delights in using us imperfect vessels. Remember, you can't follow a parked car. For these gifts to follow you, you must start moving by faith.

I. The Gift of Divers Kinds of Tongues

Every born-again believer should speak in tongues. Tongues is one of the things the Holy Spirit will manifest in a believer's life when they come to Jesus Christ and are saved (Mark 16:17). This verse mentions tongues as one of the signs that will follow believers. In devotional times, tongues can help us to pray with the mind of the Spirit, as the Spirit prays for us with more precision (Romans 8:26-27).

Speaking in tongues is a supernatural form of prayer and communion with God (1 Corinthians 14:20-25), and also a sign to unbelievers (1 Corinthians 14:20-25). When we speak in tongues, we speak in mysteries or things not understood by our natural mind, but we are edified. Our spirits are capable of communicating with God in a deep, intimate way, Spirit to spirit (John 4:24). Our spirits know things which the natural mind does not know, and receive direct revelation from God (1 Corinthians 2:11-15, 6:17 and Hebrews 4:12-13).

The ability of a believer to speak in languages normally not understood or spoken by him, is the gift of diverse kinds of tongues as explained by the Apostle Paul in the first book of 1 Corinthians 14. In order for the church to receive edification, the operation of this gift should be accompanied by the interpretation of tongues, since speaking in tongues alone will not profit the body of Christ. A person may give a message in tongues, and sometimes the interpretation will be given to another person in the group. The person who speaks in tongues should pray that God gives him the interpretation.

Not only should we be able to pray in tongues, but also to sing in tongues, in the spirit, according to 1 Corinthians 14:15. Messages in tongues should be given one at a time, in order and by two or three people, and each message should be interpreted so that the body of Christ is edified (verse 27). If there is no interpreter present, the person with the gift of tongues should hold his peace, speaking only to himself and God. Just like prophesying, speaking in tongues should not be forbidden (verse 39).

When the gift of diverse kinds of tongues operates through you, you may experience unusual spiritual and physical sensations which alert you to the fact that something is coming. You may become aware, well before the time, that God wants to give a message. Wait for the right time in the service to deliver the message.

J.   The Gift of Interpretation of Tongues

This gift is the ability given by the Holy Spirit to speak in the native language understood by the speaker, the meaning of words previously spoken in a language he did not know. It bears saying that this gift of interpretation of tongues is not the gift of translation of tongues. This will help avoid much confusion and skepticism concerning the operation of this gift. The message in tongues may be very long, and yet the interpretation will be very short, or vice versa, the message very short, and the interpretation very long.

The key word is *interpretation*. Also, two different people may interpret the same message in a very different way, and yet both have the same meaning. None of this discredits the operation of the gift. The person with this gift of interpretation of tongues will be influenced by his vocabulary and his personality or usual way of speaking. God will not override his vocabulary to give him words he has never learned.

The interpretation will be accommodated to the human vessel through whom it will be delivered. Some may interpret in a very cool, matter-of-fact manner; others will be very emotional. It may vary depending upon who the interpreter is. Some will use the English similar to the King James Version, because this is the language to which they are used to associating the voice of God.

There is nothing wrong with this, although it does not have to be given in the King James Version English. It may be given in the normal, everyday, English language we hear on the streets, so we must be flexible in this. The gift of diverse kinds of tongues, together with the interpretation of tongues, is equivalent to the gift of prophecy (1 Corinthians 14:5). Just like prophecy, the purpose of interpretation of tongues is to edify the church (verse 26), and should work in conjunction with the gift of diverse kinds of tongues to interpret the messages.

4

YOU HAVE A SPIRITUAL GIFT

A. Clearing Some Misunderstandings

One of the greatest tragedies confronting the church today is the fact that very few believers are exercising their gifts which they received from the Lord in their lives. The reason for this stems from either the fact that they ignore that they have at least one spiritual gift from their heavenly Father, or because they seem to think spiritual gifts can only operate through those who are exceptionally spiritual, and thus, worthy of the gift.

But this is an erroneous belief. The church at Corinth is proof that the possession of gifts is not to be equated with maturity or perfection in the life of the believers there (1 Corinthians 3:1-4; 5:1-13). A gift says nothing about the character of the believer; it only reveals the character of the giver. A gift is just that, a gift; it is not deserved or earned, or it would not be a gift.

Since many believers think that the gifts of the Spirit can only operate in the life of one who is spiritually mature, of sterling character, and perfect in every way, they reject any operation of a gift through anyone who does not measure up to these qualifications. Then, when in their view, the gifts operate through a person, they tend to idolize that individual as one who is far advanced spiritually, and he may be, but then again, this is the difference between gifts and fruit.

The gifts of the Spirit are given freely, regardless of spiritual maturity. They are no evidence that the person operating them has advanced spiritually. The fruit of the Spirit (Galatians 5:22-23) gives evidence of spiritual maturity. It tells us something about the person's character and their spiritual condition. Not so the gifts of the Spirit. They tell nothing about the person's character or spirituality. The validity of a gift is not determined so much by examining the life of the person through whom it operates, but it is determined by comparing its message with the Word of God and what it produces (1 Corinthians 14:3, 12, 29).

Because you are a member of God's family, you have at least one gift. This gift gives you a place and function in the body. There is no one member in your physical body without a specific function it performs. This is very important because many don't believe they have a spiritual gift, and this prevents them from ever using the gift they were given (1 Corinthians 12:7-27).

The apostle Peter also confirms the fact that there is no one who has not received a gift to minister to someone else. Everyone is called to be a steward of the grace of God. That means that we are to properly handle the gifts given to us by God (1 Peter 4:10-11).

In Romans 12:3-8, Paul says that every member of the body of Jesus Christ has a motivational gift which serves as his primary vehicle for ministry. Everyone has at least one spiritual gift which compliments or helps to do that motivational gift or ministry. Therefore, the ministry or motivational gift you have received from the Lord, according to Romans 12:3-8, will often be expressed through and/or assisted by the spiritual gift.

The spiritual gift you have will, in all probabilities, serve to administer that motivational gift (ministry), and will help you identify it and activate it in your own life. There are many self-discovery surveys available that will help you to determine which motivational gift you have. Look for one that you feel comfortable with, and do it.

B. How to Identify Your Spiritual Gift

There are three major keys to identifying the spiritual gift God has given you. They are desire, ability and confirmation (Ephesians 2:10, Philippians 2:13, 1 Timothy 1:18). Paul tells Timothy to stir up the gift of God which is in him by the putting on of his hands (2 Timothy 1:6). First, realize that God puts or gives desires in us to will. In other words, we are incapable of doing any good thing (Romans 3:12). Since it would be a good thing to desire spiritual things, we can be sure that this desire is not of ourselves; it is of God. He put that desire in us. If God has placed a burden on you to do something in the house of God, follow that burden. The Lord will anoint what He gives you the burden and passion for. If you try doing to something that you have absolutely no desire or burden for, you will never have God's anointing on your ministry. Stick to your area of anointing.

Secondly, God works in us to give us the ability "to do" that which He gives us the desire "to will to do." God will never give us the desire to do something that He will not give us the ability to do. Therefore, if you have a specific desire related to spiritual gifts, you can be sure that desire was given to you by God. If He has given you the desire for a certain gift, He will surely give you the ability to minister this gift or gifts. Paul said to covet earnestly the best gifts, and desire spiritual gifts (1 Corinthians 12:31, 14:1). There is nothing wrong about desiring spiritual gifts. That desire was put there by God, and is supported by His Word.

The third thing is confirmation of the particular gift God has given you. This means that if God has truly given you a spiritual gift or gifts, you will not be the only one who knows it. It will be confirmed by others who recognize that the operation of the gifts through you is genuine. In the case of Timothy, the gift given to him was confirmed by the laying on of Paul's hands and by the prophecies which were given to him. What gifts are you most interested in? The desire for these gifts was placed in you by God. In my experience, I have found out that there are certain characteristics in people that are conducive to certain gifts and ministries.

For example, a person with a fiery temper usually will be used in the ministry of deliverance and miracles. A person who is very sensitive or intuitive will be used in the word of knowledge, and the discerning of spirits. While the individual who is methodical and well organized is usually used in teaching and administration.

Someone gifted with the ability to express himself will flow well in the gift of prophecy and the preaching of the

Word. While someone who likes to teach, feels very comfortable with people, is patient and has a desire to protect and fuss over people will usually do well as a pastor. You will identify what ministry or gift you have received from God by being good at it and enjoy doing it.

Are you interested in these gifts to use them to minister edification to others, or is the motive one of personal glory or acclaim? (I Corinthians 14:12). We must beware of wrong desires based on pride or greed. God will not reward selfish desires (James 4:3). However, if your motives are pure and you desire to be used of God to help hurting people, even if no fame or wealth comes to you as a result of it, God will use you in the gifts of the Holy Spirit to minister to the hurting. Great will be your reward on that day at the judgment seat of Christ.

You need to be patient and understand that if the calling and gifting you have is real, no one and nothing can take it away from you. It is yours and no can cash in on it. In time, it will make a way for you. No one has the same combination of talents, abilities, personality and calling as you do. You are unique, original and there is no one like you in the whole wide world. Do not compare yourself to anyone else because it may cause one of two things and neither one is good:

1. If you look better in your own eyes compared to some one else, it will puff you up and breed pride and arrogance; a recipe for disaster in the long run.

2. If you look worse in your own eyes compared to others, you may feel discouraged and even depressed. This will not be conducive to developing your gifts and talents and may be a stumbling block in your ministry.

Start small, doing the little things where no one is watching you. Remember that servant hood is a quality that you need to develop in your life. Serve those the Lord has placed over you and in time, God will raise you up and use you in a great way. Ask God to send you a mentor, a spiritual father to coach you and train you and submit to him. It will help you immensely and save you untold heartache and pain, while shaving years off your learning and development process.

5

OPERATING IN THE
GIFTS OF THE SPIRIT

A. Getting Started

Before we get into each spiritual gift, we need to share some principles which will help you in developing spiritual gifts. One of the reasons many believers are reluctant to enter into the supernatural realm of the spirit and be used in the spiritual gifts is that they do not want to make mistakes. They want to be sure that the manifestation of any spiritual gift is done perfectly from the start. These attitudes will most certainly prevent you from entering into the realm of the spiritual gifts and operating in them.

You must understand that the gifts of the Spirit flow through frail and imperfect human vessels, which are prone to make mistakes and errors. You will learn to operate in the realm of the spirit, flowing in the gifts more perfectly as you do it more and more. This is not to say that you can learn to use a spiritual gift by natural ability, but we can more perfectly learn how to yield to the Spirit and how to discern what the Spirit is saying. As a matter of fact, a part of learning these things is making mistakes, for when you do make mistakes, you will learn how the Holy Spirit does not lead or work.

You don't have to fear that God will be angry with you if you sincerely desire, and in good faith attempt to be used in spiritual gifts. In fact, He will reward the faith of any person who attempts to yield to Him in this area. Like a baby learning to walk, you are going to fall and make mistakes while you learn to perfect the spiritual gifts that God has placed in your life. God will pick you up when you stumble, and send you on your way again.

Your attempts do not displease God. He is happy to see His children attempting to walk in His Spirit.

When a person believes the Holy Spirit is moving on him to operate in some gift, it is important that he respond immediately. The more he hesitates, the more unlikely it is that he will ever move. The natural mind will begin to find reasons why the prompting could not be God. Pride will jump in, fear will follow, and you will say to yourself, "What if I am wrong?" The quicker you respond to the leading of the Spirit, the more frequent the Spirit will move on you, and the better quality of operation of the gifts. There is a spiritual principle at work here, like in other areas of life, which rewards faithfulness in small things by giving us bigger and better things.

B. Some Practical Observations

While a person should respond immediately to the moving of the Holy Spirit, it is also important "not to rush." It is impossible to rush the Holy Spirit. If you do this, you will soon move into the area of the flesh. The best thing to do is relax and not be distracted. Even as a plane breaks the sound barrier and the ride becomes smoother, likewise when you plug into the spirit you will notice the difference as things start to flow smoothly.

Ministry becomes so much easier because you are under the anointing. As you minister, you need to keep your eyes open. Nowhere in the Bible does it say anything about closing your eyes when you are ministering to others. A person who keeps his eyes open, and asks the person receiving ministry to look upon him as he ministers, will be able to observe the effect of the ministry on the person being ministered to.

Just like Peter and John did in Acts 3:4, much can be discerned by looking into the eyes of the person receiving ministry. Is the person receiving it in faith? Is he skeptical? Is there something else hidden that the person has not said? The light of the body is in the eye, Jesus said, and much of the inner man manifests through the eyes. You must also be sensitive to the promptings of the Holy Spirit. Let the gifts of the Spirit flow through you as you minister to a person. The Holy Spirit prompts or leads basically in three ways:

1. A revelation may be seen - That is, the person operating in the gifts may see something in the spirit. If he or she is to give a message in tongues, he may "see" the words he is to speak, as if printed on a scroll or a page or several other ways. If the discerning of spirits is manifesting, he may "see" the diseased part of the body, perhaps like a dark area covering it. If the word of knowledge is operating, he may see the person to whom he is ministering in a certain situation, in a certain place, or doing something.

2. A revelation may be heard - The same way a person sees something in the spirit realm, he may hear it. This may be in the form of an audible voice, but most probably an inner voice. Words or thoughts will come, unbidden, into a person's mind to give him ministry direction. If the word of knowledge is operating, a name or place suddenly appears in his mind. When this happens, act immediately. As that information is given, the Spirit may supply additional information.

You will never know if it is from God until you step out in faith and do it. If you are unsure about it, you may say something like: "I may be wrong, but I believe the Lord is saying..." If it is of God, it will be confirmed. If not, nothing is lost and a lesson is learned. If the gift of tongues and interpretation is operating, the person may "hear" the words audibly or mentally. If the gift of healing is operating, names of diseases may suddenly come to mind. The more you respond to these messages, the more clearly and easily you will be able to distinguish the voice of the Spirit.

3. A revelation may be felt - This seems to occur mostly when ministering the gifts of healings. The person ministering may feel the pain of the individual being ministered to. This may enable him to pinpoint the location and nature of the sickness, which will tend to build faith in the sick person, or when ministering to someone under great depression, the person ministering may suddenly, and without any reason, feel depressed.

The person ministering should not be quick to accept the symptoms as his own, for it may well be the Holy Spirit's way of giving information about the person receiving ministry. Ask those present if there is someone who is experiencing the symptoms that you are feeling in your own body. Proceed slowly; take your time to make sure you are operating with the mind of Christ.

C. Some Keys to Operate Successfully

As you minister healing to a person, unless God reveals the problem to you, you need to ask the person what is wrong with him, how long he has had the problem, whether any doctor diagnosed the condition, and if there is any pain. These questions will provide you with important information that will allow you to pray more effectively. As the individual talks to you, learn to listen between the lines for signs of whether the sickness is caused by demons and requires deliverance. As you conduct the interview, be sensitive to the Spirit forany information that will enable you to pray more specifically.

When you feel that you know enough about the problem, then you can proceed to select the proper form of prayer. As mentioned above, keep your eyes open as you pray, and watch for any signs of God's power flowing through the person being ministered to. You may feel God's virtue flow through your hands. In our ministry, when we pray for sick folk, I feel heat and God's virtue flowing through my hands into the person's body.

This does not have to happen in order for a person to be healed. Sometimes, I do not feel anything and people still are healed. As you are praying, stop and ask the person what is happening to him, and what he is feeling. This will give you an idea of what God is doing, and help you to decide what to do next.

After the praying phase is over, quickly ask the person being ministered to if there is any pain. The absence of pain usually indicates that a healing has taken place. However, there may still be some stiffness or weakness in the limb. These symptoms will usually go away with time, as the body parts are used. You may also ask them to do something that they could not do before. This will confirm the healing.

Sometimes people may be slain in the spirit when you pray over them. While they are on the floor, do not disturb them. This is God's anesthesia while He is performing the operation. Let Him finish what He is doing. After they get up, ask them all the questions you want. Most of the time, you will be pleasantly surprised to find out that a miracle has taken place if you let God finish what He started.

After you pray, if nothing happens you need to assess and reevaluate the situation. Further questioning is necessary to determine the true source of the problem, and the type of prayer needed. Most doctors agree that the majority of diseases are psychosomatic. This means that they have their origin in the mind or the emotions, and eventually starts affecting their bodies. Maybe there is bitterness, resentment and un-forgiveness that need to be resolved. If so, lead the person in a prayer of forgiveness, sharing with them the need to forgive.

If still nothing happens, and you suspect the person may need deliverance, (and there is a deliverance ministry team available to help the person), ask the person if he would like to receive ministry in deliverance. If the person wants deliverance, schedule a ministry time with them (see next section). If there is no deliverance ministry available, tell them about the love of God, how much He cares for them, and schedule another time when you may pray for them again. Most of the time, a person will be grateful for the time you took to pray for them and for the love you showed them.

However, under no circumstances should you tell anyone that they do not have enough faith, or that they have done something wrong, or put any other kind of guilt or condemnation upon them. This will only destroy their faith, and they will leave much worse than when they came to you. If sin or a wrong lifestyle is responsible for the person's sickness, talk to them about breaking those habits, and developing a healthier lifestyle.

D. Deliverance Ministry

This ministry should not be attempted by anyone unless the person believes the Lord has called him to this ministry, and has been trained properly by someone experienced in deliverance ministry. You must be walking close to the Lord, and living a life of purity if you are going to be a part of the deliverance ministry team. This ministry should only be attempted after at least one or more experienced ministers determine that a particular person may need deliverance.

This brief section is by no means meant to cover the difficult and controversial subject of deliverance ministry or train anyone in it. There are some other books and materials you may obtain that will help you in this area. We also conduct seminars in churches to train people in deliverance ministry specifically, and other areas as well. We are barely going to mention a few things that may suggest a person may need deliverance. Sometimes there are some visible manifestations in people as you minister to them, which could possibly indicate demonic infestation such as:

1. A mental block – the person has a hard time answering questions and talking about a certain topic.

2. Incoherent talk – Without warning, the individual starts talking nonsense, things that have nothing to do with what is going on.

3. Hatred or glassy, unfocused eyes – When you press a trigger point in the person, he may react with some form of hateful, bitter comment, causing his eyes to become unfocused and glassy looking.

4. Shortness of breath – When this happens, it is usually a sign that that something has been stirred up inside the individual, and may manifest any moment.

5. Blasphemy – The individual will start to say cuss words and blasphemies for no apparent reason.

6. Violent reactions such as screams, kicks and blows – If it gets to that, you can be pretty sure that this person needs some serious deliverance. It is always good to have some strong arms available just in case.

7. Retching and vomiting – This is a clear indication that the person is demonized, and demons need to be cast out of him. Do not make the mistake of attempting to do it all by yourself. Share with the person that you belief he may need deliverance, and the need to schedule a meeting with a minister experienced in this area.

6

UNDERSTANDING
DREAMS AND VISIONS

A. Introduction

There is something very special about God speaking to you in your dreams and through visions. This is one of the ways that God communicates with each of us, and is made abundantly clear by the numerous times it happens in the Bible (Job 33:14-16; Acts 17:27-28). The reason that dreams and visions are more common is because sight is our strongest sense of all. Dreams and visions can help us to solve problems, warn us of impending danger, guide us and help us fulfill God's will for our lives.

Learning to interpret dreams and visions is important because of the impact they may have on our lives. Doing so requires that we understand the language of heaven, and that dreams are *highly symbolic*. There are only two ways that there is an uninterrupted outward flow from within your spirit, towards you soul and into your mind: asleep, unconscious or when your senses are in a spirit of suspension so that you ignore them. That is the only time when your senses are not active. Only when you still your senses can things from within your spirit begin to pour out and come into your mind.

This is what dreams and visions are. Dreams are influences that come up out of your spirit while you are asleep. So during dreams, your spirit is able to start to communicate things outwardly. Your spirit will communicate this information to your mind in the same way as information coming to your mind from the outside: through the five senses. These are the only things that your mind is able to understand.

If you received a dream that you believe is prophetic, first write it down. Then begin to speak in tongues, keeping the dream in mind. As you continue to speak in tongues, you will receive a vision or an impression in your spirit. Maybe someone or something will come to your mind. Now try to describe what you are seeing or feeling in the spirit in your own language.

If you see a vision that you do not understand, do not worry. Continue to pray in tongues while keeping the picture in your mind. You might see the vision change or see another one. Always speak words of faith, hope and love. Do not be afraid to speak things directly into the atmosphere like: "I speak blessing on the finances; I speak healing; I call it done". There is power in your words.

One major mistake that people make in interpreting dreams is thinking that people we dream about actually represent themselves. In reality, many times they *represent a part of you*. For example if you dream about y*our boss*, he might represent *your work or your relationships at work*. If you dream about your father or someone you respect and honor, it is possible he *represents the Lord* in your dreams. If you *dream of an (ex)*, they *could speak of the flesh*. *Your mother could speak of your relationship with your church. Children* usually have to do with *your ministry, visions or goals-things you have birthed.*

These are just some of the things the Holy Spirit may give you, but ask Him to give you revelation. Just doing this, your dreams will begin to make sense to you. Make a list of the characters that you often dream about, and next to the name of each person, write down a short description of what your relationship is with that person. When you think about them, what is the first thing that comes to mind? Let's learn how to identify objects and flow better in prophetic dreams.

B. Hearing God through Dreams

Sometimes, it seems that there is so much noise, chatter and interference going on around us and in our mind, that it makes it very hard to hear the voice of the Lord clearly. We are going to learn how to clear up some of that noise, and come to a place where you can start hearing the Lord better than you ever have before.

1. You Can Hear From the Lord

Are you a Christian? Is Jesus living in your heart? Then you can hear His voice (Joel 2:28; Mathew 7:7-8). The Lord wants you to know that He's saying more than you want to hear it. His greatest desire is to communicate with you. He wants you to know Him intimately; to give you direction in your life and for you to be blessed. When you know these truths, you already have prepared the way to hear His voice better.   Now even though you have a desire to hear from the Lord, there is no doubt something blocking you. There could be various reasons like lack of a good relationship with the Lord, sin, pride, lack of obedience, mistreating your mate, but let's deal with the main one.

You see, when the Lord speaks to you, He speaks to you from your own spirit. He does not shout down from heaven, or sends messages in spiritual blimps. You must remember a simple principle. What you put into your spirit will determine what will come out. What is the word the Lord is giving you having to filter through? Think for a moment what you have read, listened to and the activities you have engaged in just this week. If any of these things have been restoring and feeding your spirit, you are probably going to have prophetic dreams coming easily to you. However, if you have filled your spirit with worldly things, then you are going to have to do some digging to remove that junk first.

The best and easiest way to get results is to speak in tongues and to get into the Word. By refreshing your mind, your spirit will begin to get rid of everything that is blocking it. Try speaking in tongues every single day for as long as you are able to. Read the Word every single day and try to visualize what you are reading. See the pictures in your mind of what you are reading. Soon your spirit will be alive in a way it never has before.

2. Receiving through Dreams

In your dreams you see, hear, taste, smell and touch things. There is no other way that your spirit can communicate outward through your mind except through the senses. As you dream, you need to identify what is being communicated to you through the five senses. What did you see, hear, taste, feel and smell? All these things are coming out to communicate a message to you. Your spirit cannot speak to your mind in words, with an audible voice. The only way it can speak is through the five senses, and the most common sense is always the sense of sight. Images are powerful. Remember that one single picture can say a thousand words (*For dream symbols see Appendix A*).

Write the dreams down as soon as you wake up. I have learned that you forget dreams quickly if you do not write them down. Also, you should date them and title them for future reference. Most of your dreams are going to be pictures, things you see. What comes up out of your spirit in dreams, will take several forms:

a.   The Father

If you are dreaming about your father, that character in your dream represents a part of you that typifies your relationship with your heavenly Father. Do you have a good relationship with your earthly father? Do you look up to him and respect him? Is he your covering and protection and someone you admire? If that is true, then your father could be a picture of the Lord in your dream. Think back on any dream that you had with your father in it. Was he instructing you, leading you or trying to tell something in your dream?

If you have a bad relationship with your father, it could mean something different which you must assess yourself. It might represent your flesh, or the tendency to walk in sin. Please bear in mind that this symbolism will change with each person. It is a known scientific fact among psychiatrists and psychologists that people associate the image they have of their earthly fathers to God.

By assessing your relationship with your father, you will also get a good indication of how you see the Lord. The role of the father in the home is to represent the Lord to his family. If your father failed to represent the Lord correctly, then the image you have of the Lord may be distorted and erroneous.

b. The Mother

If you have a good relationship with your mother, then she will often represent the church in your dreams. As the bride of your father, she will also speak of the Bride of Christ. In this case, dreams that have your mother in it will likely address your role in the church and your views toward other believers.

If your relationship with your mother is bad, then she may represent something else in your life, like flesh, weaknesses or any other characteristic that may aptly define her. However, always seek revelation from the Lord concerning confirmation on what the symbols in your dreams represent.

c. Spouse

If you are dreaming about your spouse, it depends what kind of relationship you have. If it is good and your spouse is a good influence in your life, harmony, closeness, your spouse could be a picture of your spirit or the H.S. If your spouse is standing in the way of your spiritual progress all the time, it could be a picture of the flesh, an obstacle, something that gets in the way. Assess it yourself.

d. Family Members

If the characters in your dream are family members like brothers and sisters, it will depend what kind of relationship you have with them. If you dream about your children, likely they are a picture of those things you have given birth to. They may be a picture of spiritual ministry, or of spiritual fruit in your life. Depending on what your child did in your dream, it would tell me something about your life.

e. First Love

Whenever you dream about the first person you ever fell in love with, God is usually speaking about your relationship with Him. There are so many different characters coming into your dream that you are going to need to understand what each of them means to you. Only you can accurately interpret internal dreams because it is all about you.

f. Vehicles and Movement

If in your dreams you are running away from beasts and monsters that are chasing you, it is picture of conflict in your spiritual life. If you dream of vehicles, it depends what they mean to you. Usually a vehicle is a picture of movement or activity in life. To some people, it is a picture of their ministry.

g. Male and Female Characters

Dreams can tell you if there is a negative influence in your life. If in your dreams a male or female character appears that you seem to be familiar with, but cannot recognize or identify, it often speaks about your masculine and feminine qualities in you. Over time, you will eventually be able to tell what your spirit is trying to say as it comes into your mind during your dreams. For a complete list of symbol interpretation in dreams, please see *Appendix A.*

C. Internal and External Dreams

Dreams take in two main forms; the first is what is known as an *internal dream.* In this kind of dream, most of the things in it are symbolic, and generally refers to the person having the dream. This means that everything that you see in the dream is not really what it appears to be. When this happens, you need to understand what you are seeing. The Bible is full of symbols, and as we walk through life, we encounter symbols as well. We associate certain objects with certain things, and the scriptures do as well.

For example, the Holy Spirit if often typified by oil or by water. We also have the Lamb of God, speaking of His gentleness and humility. The Lion of Judah speaks of strength and power. Trees usually refer to people and the fig tree, specifically to Israel. There are many symbols in the Bible, so when our spirit communicates with us through dreams, it does so through these pictures. Here is where many people miss their dreams. Dreams are filled often with characters and places that you know in real life. They are pictures that your mind fed into your spirit. As your spirit begins to communicate with your mind, it looks for materials and events stored there. It puts on a little plays for you, so it looks for props, characters and actors.

1. Internal Dreams

An internal dream pertains to you alone. It has to do with your current spiritual condition, where you are in ministry, your relationship with the Lord or something in your life. This dream functions very much like the word of knowledge in that it relates to the past and present, and therefore may have to do with something you have encountered in the past, will encounter in the future or both. But how do you identify an internal dream? *It is the dream where you are the main character, the star.* You are actively involved with the characters in the dream, and the activity revolves around you. This is an indication that your dream is internal and has to do with something in your life or something you will encounter. People make a common mistake that when they have a dream that they think is from God and the characters and objects relate to real people. This can get real scary and confusing especially if you dream that someone you know has died.

When you realize that your dream is internal and the people and objects in your dreams are symbolic, it opens a whole new world of understanding to you. Someone dying might not always be a bad thing. It might mean a part of your life has died. It might indicate a new start in your life. You might dream of giving birth, which often indicates the birth of a new ministry or opportunity in your life. Most of the time you are the star of it, and you are right in the middle of it. When you take a part in your dream this is usually an internal dream. That means that the dream is about you. It is not about somebody else, it is about you. The characters that you see in your dream are not actually the people you see. They are simply character that have been picked to symbolize an aspect of your life. So your dream is your life. It is your life being portrayed in a play.

You did not know you could write plays, but your spirit is very good at it. If you are going to understand your dream, you are going to have to look at the whole picture. You need to look at the stage, and at the background. Take a look at the scene that is being portrayed. Look at the colors involved. You need to look at the people involved. Are they close to you? Are they strangers? What objects appear in your dream? Do you see vehicles? Do you see the sun, the moon and stars that are a part of life? Each of these things is a symbol or picture of you, your life, ministry & your spirit is trying to give you a message, to let you know what is going on in your life.

Internal dreams are usually not prophetic in nature. They are not a prediction. They are not something that you need to share with the world. Internal dreams are not shared with the church because it is not about the church, or other people, the dream is about you. This is where many times people get confused. They assume that since they had a clear dream, it was obvious that God was speaking to them, and must be prophetic.

Many assume it is for the church, or for somebody else. They begin to interpret the dream based on others, when all the time God is trying to gain their attention, and say something to them personally. It may be trying to give you a warning, a promise, hope. Whatever the dream is trying to do, it is for you and not somebody else. If you are going to be able to interpret your dream, you will have to learn to interpret symbols remembering that the symbols in your dream relate to you alone.

2. External Dreams

These dreams are more prophetic. If the dreams are recurring, they deserve special attention. In these dreams, you are usually observing everything from a place or platform where you see everything taking place, but no one sees you. These are the dreams when the characters represent real characters in life. But here is the tricky part; it is sometimes difficult to know when you are having an internal or external dream. You may for example dream of somebody close to you dying, and you may think *"God is warning me that my husband is going to die"*. Actually it could be saying that the things that you are married to are going to die. A thing that may be standing in the way of your spiritual progress and God is going to take remove them from your life. It could actually be a very good dream. But an external dream is when the characters in your dream become real characters. The places you see in your dreams are real places, they are not symbolic anymore. You need to start understanding and interpreting what they mean.

3. Difference between Internal and External Dreams

The best way to tell the difference between internal and external dreams is to notice whether you are the star of the dream, or you are watching it from the outside. If your dream is as though you are looking at it on a TV, or you are just a bystander looking at it, but not actually involved in it, that sometimes is an indication that your dream is external. If you are not actively involved in the dream or one of the key players, then your dream is starting to move more into the external. You are likely looking at something that is more prophetic; the characters in the dream may be real.

Perhaps it could be God revealing things about a person or about your relationship with that person. But external dreams or prophetic dreams are really a vision given during sleep. It is what the scripture calls a *night vision*, a vision given while you are asleep. You need to remember that 90% of the dreams most people dream are not external dreams, they are internal. Everybody dreams, but you start moving into the prophetic realm, only then you start receiving night visions. Sometimes, it is possible that your dream is both internal and external.

4. Dreams That Are both Internal and External

These are the dreams where you are a part of the dream, but the dream has to do with something or someone other than yourself. These dreams may have an indirect impact on your life. When we look at the interpretation that Daniel gave the king concerning the dreams he had, we see that they had two interpretations. The first time he interpreted the king's dream he interpreted it as external, but actually it had an internal meaning as well. When the king saw the image of the stone that shattered the image, it was God warning King Nebuchadnezzar that He was going to break him and humble him. Daniel maybe did not have the courage to tell the king the internal, personal meaning, so he gave him the external, prophetic meaning.

Later on the king had another dream where an angel comes down from heaven and cuts down the tree, and hears a voice speak about this person with dew over his head for seven years. Daniel tells the king that the dream is basically about him. This is a personal internal dream that God is speaking to the person now. In this case, it is more than an internal dream; it is actually an internal prophetic dream. So when it comes to interpreting dreams, you need to learn how to distinguish the two or you will be confused.

5. Healing and Purging Dreams

Finally, there is another kind of dream which is neither internal nor external. It is not prophetic, nor is it a message. It is just absolute garbage, rubbish. You may think that maybe it was because of what you had for dinner before you went to bed. You dream stuff a Christian should not dream. You feel unclean in the morning when you wake up. You blame the devil, and say he attacked you during the night. Although that is possible and it does happen, usually it is something else. Sometimes you feel pain, joy and emotions; fighting somebody although in real life you may not be the kind of person who fights much. In your dreams you may be suffering severe temptation and giving in to lust. What is happening is all the garbage that you have picked up and accumulated in the world is simply being purged out.

You see, everything that you receive while you are awake is fed inwards through the five senses into your subconscious mind. Normally, this is what regulates the lives of people. However, when you have the Spirit of God within you, He begins to purge it out. As you begin to fill yourself with the Word of God, pray more and get more into the things of God, your dreams may become worse for a while. What is actually happening, is the word is getting into your heart and displacing all the junk out. It is like the bottom of a lake that has been standing still for a long time; and the water is crystal clear and beautiful. All the junk and garbage that has deposited in the lake over a period of time, has been covered over with a fine layer of sand and it appears smooth, clean and fine.

However, if you go to the edge of the lake and put a stick in it and start to stir the bottom, all the filth that is lying down there is stirred up and starts coming out. The sea cleanses itself like this all the time. That is why, when you take a walk on the seashore in the morning, you will see all the flotsam, weeds, garbage and debris. That is what happens when you have healing dreams.

The Holy Spirit and the Word of God is going to stir the stuff lying dormant in your subconscious mind, causing it to come out as garbage and horrible dreams; but they are actually healing dreams. If you have dreams where you relive painful, hurtful experiences, what is really happening is that your spirit is purging all those bad memories of the past. Now the Holy Spirit can come in and replace it with the Word of God and good things.

You need to learn to discern what is coming from your dreams, and to hear the voice of God; whether it is giving you an instruction or a warning; or maybe a prophetic word for somebody else. Depending on what your dreams reveal, you will be given a course of action to take.

D. Visions

Not too long ago, it seemed unthinkable that every single believer would have access to the Lord and be able to speak with Him. However, now we are training the emerging army of the Lord so they can hear God for themselves, and learn to know how He speaks through dreams and visions. Interpreting your dreams is just one way the Lord can speak to you, but now I want to guide you into learning a bit more about visions.

For many people, when they think of having a vision they imagine that it is a super spiritual experience. But the truth is that visions are very simply pictures that come unbidden into your mind. In fact, you may have already been having visions for a long time. This is something that you can experience right now, and it is so simple, that you might overlook it because visions do not always come in the same way or the same form.

1.   What Is a Vision?

A vision is simply an influence coming up out of your spirit into your mind. The difference is that is takes place while you are awake. It is really just a dream while you are awake. A lot of people have visions without realizing it. If you really desire to be able to flow more in visions, there are some things you must do before. You are going to learn how to be receptive to visions, and you will begin to have visions depending on the level of prophetic anointing that rests upon your life.

2.   How to Receive Visions

First, you need to just settle your spirit. If there is noise going on around you, then wait until it is quiet. Submit yourself to the Lord and ask Him to speak to you. Then close your eyes. When you do this, many thoughts will come to your mind. You will see various flashes and images come to you. Let the pictures just roll. You might see scenes from a movie you watched or an event that happened today.

As these various images flash through your mind, you will start to see pictures that do not tie in with things you have watched. They are not the kind of pictures that you would have made up. This same picture will pop up into your mind a few times. It is gentle and might not even be totally clear at first. Now, do not be afraid that you might be deceived. Be bold. Step forward and allow the Holy Spirit to speak to you.

3.   Trance Visions

When a trance takes place, our natural senses are placed into a state of suspension. It is an influence so strong, that the natural senses are suspended so that you do not see or hear anything that is going on about you. You are taken up with the vision just like you would be with a dream. Most people do not have trance visions. If you are a prophet and you have not had a trance vision, do not worry about it. It could just mean that you are able to hear from your spirit being without having to be knocked out. It is the same with being slain in the spirit. Some people can receive without being slain in the spirit, others have to be zapped. This is like God's anesthetic. Some people do not need anesthetic and are open enough to the Spirit of God that He can speak and they are able to hear Him without loosing consciousness.

4. Picture Visions

Not every vision comes in the form of plays or movies. Sometimes they are just still photos or slides that are imprinted in your mind. This is still a vision and comes up from within your spirit. Every one, not just prophets, have the ability to receive these types of picture visions. If you would just close your eyes, calm your thoughts and let your mind go freely as you start to love and worship the Lord, you will be surprised by the stuff that comes up into your mind. I experience this sometimes as I go to sleep at night. It is like I start dreaming before I fall sleep. This is coming from the same place our dreams come from, from deep within us.

Many pictures, symbols, revelation from the Lord will come to you like that. Try it sometimes when you are praying; get a pen and paper and ask the Lord to speak to you. Then write down every picture, symbol, vision, thought, anything that comes up into your mind. You will be amazed as you look back how many of them have spiritual significance and could be interpreted just like our dreams. This is God speaking to you internally through your spirit. As you learn to develop this, recognize it and shut out what is going on around you as you receive the pictures coming from deep within you *(See Appendix A)*.

You will learn to do it while you are praying for somebody in intercession, or praying for people. You will eventually learn to develop it where your inner vision becomes so clear and distinct, as if you were having a dream. Some people can see visions so clear and distinct because they are able to simply shut out the external influences and draw into themselves. These are people who are introverts. They tend to be loners and keep to themselves. They live in their thoughts and live in a daydream world a lot. They have developed this capacity of living in a fantasy world. These people usually have the ability to receive a vision and turn off everything going on around them. Learn to shut it out as you start seeing the visions coming up from within you.

5. Open Visions

There us another kind of vision that is more powerful because it overrides our natural senses. It is what the Bible calls open vision. Open vision is when you can look at your surroundings and you are suddenly seeing something else superimposed on your surroundings. Some people, who have a vision of the Lord, have this type of vision. They have seen an angel standing next to them, or somewhere in the same room.

They see everything around them normal, but superimposed on top of that is the vision they are having. That is an open vision and it varies depending on the person, and how sensitive they are. It depends on how you can shut out your senses, and whether God has to knock you out or not. You receive these types of influences in your mind in dreams and visions.

E. Some Practical Observations

When you come to God in prayer, spend some time listening to Him. Here are some suggestions:
1. Come into His presence with music
2. Make sure there are no distractions around you
3. Rest in His presence; be comfortable and relaxed
4. Ask the Lord to reveal Himself and speak to you
5. You might see some words and pictures start coming into your mind *(See Appendix A)*.
6. Do not stop there. Speak to the Lord as you feel led, but also be aware of your senses.
7. Are you receiving any sensory information? Like smell, taste, hearing, vision? Understand these things will be coming from your spirit
8. When you take time to hear from the Lord, you will get to love Him more and know Him better. Learn to be a lover of Jesus; your best and closest friend. He is the lover of your soul. Treasure your time with Him.

Appendix A

Dreams & Visions Interpretation

ANIMALS

Ant:
Industrious
Worker
Wisdom
Preparation
Diligence

Ass:
Patience
Endurance
Stubbornness
Self will

Bear:
Evil men
Danger
Cunning
Cruel men

Beast:
Worldly Kingdoms
Cruel
Devouring

Bees:
Busy Bodies
Gossip
Group of people
Produces honey
Stings

Bird:
Clean or Unclean
Holy Spirit- Dove
Evil Spirit- Crow
or Raven
Holy Spirit- Eagle
Prophets- Eagle

Bull:
Strength

Labor/Servant

Calf:
Praise
Thanksgiving

Camel:
Burden Bearer
Service

Cat:
Unclean spirit
Crafty, mysterious
Personal
Sneaky
Undependable

Caterpillar:
Destruction
Devourer
Destroyer
Famine

**Crocodile,
Alligator:**
Strong expression
of demonic power

Dog:
Unbelievers
Hypocrites
Samaritans
Shunned ones
Dissension
Attack against
God's work
Demons hide in

Donkey:
Hard Headed
Endurance
Self will

Dove:
Holy Spirit
Gentleness

**Dragon,
Dinosaur:**
High level of
demonic attack
Leviathan
Spiritual
wickedness in
high places

Eagle:
Soaring in the
Spirit
Good Leader
Strength
Swiftness
Power of God
Prophets
Holy Spirit
Great Vision, Seer

Fish:
Souls of men
Clean and unclean

Flies:
Evil Spirit
Lies, Gossip,
Slander
Filth, Perversion
Satan's kingdom
Torment
Impurity
Beelzebub
demons

Fox:
Secret sins

Cunning man
Deception
Predator
FROG:
Demon spirits
Lying nature
Deception

Goat:
Carnal
Fleshly Christians
Unbelief
Christians walking
in sin
False Prophet

**Grasshopper,
Locust:**
Destroyer
Destruction
Famine,
Barrenness
Judgment
Multitudes

Hare, Rabbit:
Satan
Evil host
Uncleanness

Hart, Deer:
Gentleness
Timidity
Sensitivity
Church Leader
Thirsty Believer

Horse:
Move of God
Power
Strength
Conquest
War
Plowing, Labor

Lamb:
Jesus Christ
Sacrifice
Gentle
Innocent
Pure, Clean
True Believers

Lice:
Accusation,
Lies
Shame

Lion:
Conqueror
Overcomer
Devourer
Devil
Jesus Christ
King

Ox:
Hard worker
Sacrifice
Service
OWL:
Evil spirits
Night Bird
Wisdom
Demonic powers

Pelican:
Lonely person
Independent
Efficient worker

Ram:
Male sheep
Pride
Strength

Raven:
Evil spirit
Unclean
Scavenger

Rooster:
Warning
Reminder
Early Riser
New Beginning

Scorpion:
Evil spirit
Evil men
Pain
Injustice

Serpent:
Satan
Evil spirits
Evil men
Liar
Deceiver
Curse
Criticism
Sensual wisdom
Earthly

Sheep:
God's People

True Believer
Redeemed
Defenseless
Unsaved Person
The Church
Israel
Dull in Thinking

Spider:
False Doctrine
Weaves webs of
Deceit
Enticing demonic
presence
Wisdom
Efficiency

Stork:
Loneliness
Production

Turtle Dove:
Holy Spirit

Wild Ass:
Unregenerate
man
Stubborn
Self willed
Running Wild

Wolf:
Satan
False Teachers
False Prophet
Deception
Devourer
Plan to destroy
God's Flock
Devious, Lurking

Worm:
Instrument of
Judgment
Famine, Death
Despised
Filthiness of the
Flesh
Carnality

COLORS

Black:
Death of Old self
Mourning
Evil

Humiliation
Affliction
Calamity
Opposite of purity
Death
Famine
Sin
Ignorance

Blue:
Holy Spirit
Revelation
Divinity
Authority
Heaven
Heavenly
Visitation
Cleansing
Hope
Freedom
Healing
Grace

Brass
Judgment
Suffering
Testing

Brown:
Flesh
Carnality
Earthen
Creation
Barren

Gold, Amber:
Crowns
Divinity
Glory
Holiness
Holy Spirit
Kingship
Metal
Presence of God
Purification
Royalty
Sanctification

Gray:
Mixture
Compromise
Deception
Half Truths
Complacency
Dignity, Honor

Green:
Abundance
Envy
Eternal Life
Freshness
Fruitful
Grace
Growth
Jealousy
Life
Mercy
New Beginning
Praise
Prosperity
Resting in God
Vigor
Witchcraft

Orange:
Glory
New Age,
Mysticism
Danger, Caution
Spiritual Warfare
Praise
Intercession
Warning

Pink:
Healing
Flesh, Carnal
Heavenly Care
New Life
Power

Purple:
Authority
Covering
Kingly
Majesty
Prince
Rich
Royalty
Wealth

**Red, Crimson,
Scarlet:**
Atonement
Blood of Jesus
Bloodshed
Chariots of Fire
Cleansing
Courage
Covenant
Covering

Covetousness
Forgiveness
Holy Fire
Love
Passion
Redemption
Sacrifice
Selfishness
Sin
Strong Emotion
Suffering
Sacrifice
Salvation
War
Warfare
Zealousness

Silver:
Medals
Price
Redemption
Strength

White:
Blameless
Blood Washed
Clean
Holiness
Honor
Glory
Light
Pure
Purity
Righteousness
Robes of Saints
Righteousness
Something good
The Bride
Triumph
Victory

Yellow:
Joy
Sunshine

NUMBERS

One:
Beginning
First
New
Source
Unity

Two:
Discern
Division
Witness
Witnessing
Separation
Testimony

Three:
Body, Soul, Spirit
Complete
Divine Perfection
Godhead
Perfection
Witness

Four:
Creation
Creative Work
Earth
Four Elements
Four Seasons
Four Directions
North, East,
South, West
Wind
World

Five:
Atonement
Cross
Five fold Ministry
Grace
Ministry
Service

Six:
Beast
Carnal
Evils of Satan
Flesh
Number of man
Man without God
Man's Weakness
Satan
Sin Nature
Works of man

Seven:
Completion
Consummation
Finished Work
Perfection
Ultimate Victory

Eight:
Dying to Self

Liberty in Spirit
New Beginnings
New Birth

Nine:
Darkness
Falling short
Finality
Fruit of Spirit
Fullness
Judgment

Ten:
Covenant
Divine Order
Government
Law
Measure
Order
Perfection
Responsibility
Testimony
Testing
Tithe
Trial

Eleven:
Antichrist
Betrayal
Confusion
Disorder
Disorganization
End
Final
Finish
Incomplete
Judgment
Lawlessness

Twelve:
Apostolic Fullness
Church
Discipleship
Government
Perfection
People of God

Thirteen:
Apostasy
Backsliding
Depravity
Occult
Rebellion
Rejection
Satan
Witch Coven

Wilderness

Fourteen:
Deliverance
Salvation
Recreate,
Reproduce
Servant

Fifteen:
Deliverance
Grace
Freedom
Rest

Sixteen:
Love
Salvation

Seventeen:
Victory
Incomplete
Immature

Eighteen:
Bondage
Captivity
Judgment,
Destruction

Nineteen:
Faith
Repentance
Ashamed
Barren

Twenty:
Redemption
Time of Waiting

Twenty One:
Wickedness
Sinfulness
Corruption

Twenty Two:
Light

Twenty Three:
Death

Twenty Four:
Priesthood

Twenty Five:
Forgiveness of Sin

Twenty Six:
The Gospel

Twenty Seven:
Preaching the

74

Gospel

Twenty Eight:
Eternal Life

Twenty Nine:
Departure

Thirty:
Entering Ministry
Maturity
Blood of Christ

Thirty One:
Offspring

Thirty Two:
Covenant

Thirty Three:
Promise
Power
Resurrection

Thirty Four:
Naming a Son

Thirty Five:
Hope

Thirty Six:
Enemy

Thirty Seven:
Word of God

Thirty Eight:
Slavery

Thirty Nine:
Disease

Forty:
Probation
Trials, testing
Temptation
Judgment
One Generation

Forty One:
Deception
Misunderstood

Forty Two:
The Coming of
Jesus Christ

Forty Three:
Abomination of
Desolation

Forty Four:
Perdition

Forty Five:
Inheritance
Preservation

Forty Six:
Second Death

Forty Seven:
Calling

Forty Eight:
Tabernacle
Dwelling Place

Forty Nine:
Wrath of God
Satan's Attack

Fifty:
Pentecost
Holy Spirit
Jubilee
Liberty

Sixty:
Pride
Fullness of
Gentiles

Sixty Five:
Glory

Sixty Six:
Idol Worship

Seventy:
Restoration
Increase,
restoration
Multitude

One Hundred:
Fullness
People of Promise
God's Election
Promised Children

**One Hundred
Twenty:**
Complete
Life Span
Start of Life
End of Carnality
Power
Demonstration of
Spirit Power

**One Hundred
Forty Four:**
God's Redemption
Perfect

Government

Three Hundred:
God's Chosen
Remnant

Six Hundred:
600 Hundred
Chariots pursued
Israel
Goliath's Spear
weighed 600
shekels
Danites sent 600
men to defeat
Josiah

**Six Hundred
Sixty Six:**
Number of Satan
The beast
Bondage
Mark of the beast

One Thousand:
Maturity
Millennial Reign
Fullness of Time

Two Thousand:
Church age ends
Length of Age
**One Hundred
Forty Four
Thousand:**
Saved Humanity
God's Perfect
Government

PEOPLE

Angel:
Messenger sent
from God
Maybe a Christian
Good or bad
Protector

Baby:
Ministry
New Birth
Ministry in its
Infancy
Helpless
Untouched, Pure
New Christian

75

New Move of God
Spiritual
Immaturity

Bride:
The Church
Covenant

Brother:
The Holy Spirit
Spiritual brother
in the church
Yourself
Your Brother
Pastor

Clown, Jester:
Childish works
Works of Flesh
Playing with God
Mocker

Daughter:
Child of God
Ministry that is
your child in the
spirit
Child traits within
you
The child

Doctor:
Healer
Authority
Worldly Wisdom

Driver:
One in control of
the ministry or
marriage
Good or evil

Drunk:
Under the
influence of an
evil spirit
Controlled
Rebellion
Self Indulging
Addicting
Out of Control
Unbalanced

Employee:
Servant
Showing
submission
Protégée

Employer:
Someone in
charge
Good or bad
authority
Pastor, Leader
Mentor

Family:
Church Family
Natural Family

Farmer:
Minister
Pastor
Preacher
Evangelist

Father:
Father God
Holy Spirit
Authority
Inheritance
Tradition
Satan
Natural Father

**Foreigner,
Stranger:**
Not of the Flock
Outsider
Someone to watch

Giant:
Angel
Demon
Challenge
Mountain that
needs climbing
Strongholds to
conquer
Addictions

**Governor,
Mayor:**
Government
Person in charge
Rule and reign

Grandchild:
Someone who
came out of your
ministry
Spiritual legacy
Heir
Grandchild

Grandparent:
Spiritual
Inheritance
Past
Wisdom

Groom:
Christ
Marriage
Union
Covenant,
Promise

**Harlot,
Prostitute:**
Adultery
Temptation
Snare
Seduction
Worldly Church
Rebellious
Idolater
Compromise

Husband:
Christ
Husband
Satan
Headship
Covering

Lawyer:
Advocate
Christ
Legalism

Man:
God's Messenger
Demonic
Messenger
Evil Motive
Kind Stranger
Jesus

Mother:
Church
Jerusalem
Charity and Love
Comfort
Holy Spirit
Meddler
Mother
Birther
Trainer

Old Man:
Carnality

Wisdom
Carnal man
Adam

Pastor or Preacher:
Represents God
Wife could be the church
Spiritual Authority
From Home
Church

Police:
Spiritual Authority in Church
Pastor or Elders
Protection
Natural Authority
Angels or Demons

Sister:
Sister in Christ
Similar qualities in self
The Church
Sister
Companion

Soldier:
Spiritual Warfare
Angel
Demon warring against you
Persecution
Against

Son:
Same as Daughter except gender change
Christ
Submissive to Father

Tax man:
The Devourer
Unjust weights and scales

Teacher:
Christ Holy Spirit
Revelation of God
Teacher in Church
Important
Instruction

Thief:
Satan
Deceiver,
Dishonesty
Works of the Flesh
Judas in the ministry

Wife:
Church
Wife
Joined,
Submissive
Bride of Christ
Holy Spirit

Witch:
Rebellion
Witchcraft
Sorcery
Occult
Practices
Slander
Curses
Non-Submissive Wife
Controlling Spirit
Male and Female
Seduction
Worldly Church

Woman:
Angel
Demon
Witchcraft
Seducing Spirit
Temptation
Yourself

PLACES:

Airport:
Place of Preparation
Waiting
Change
Ready to soar in the Spirit
Training for prophets, seers

Bank:
Treasure placed in heaven
The Church

Protected
Safe, secure
Storage

Barn:
Place of provision
Church
Storage

Beauty shop:
Preparation
Holiness
Vanity
Pride

Cafeteria:
Church service
Systematic serving of the Word
Picking what you want to eat
Repetitive Ministry
Compromise

Church:
Church service
The Building
The Corporate Structure
Congregation

City:
The Church
Corporate
Known for its founder

Classroom, School:
Place of teaching
Instruction
Small groups
Teaching Ministry
Mentoring Ministry
Discipleship

Cliff, Building Ledge:
About to fall away
Danger
Take a Risk
A leap of Faith

Courthouse, Courtroom:
Time of Trial
Difficulty

Persecution
Slander
Accusations
Judgment
Being Judged
Being weighed in
the balance

Electronics Store:
Place to acquire
heavenly gifts of
hearing and
seeing
New Level of
Communications
coming to you

Factory:
Place of spiritual
productivity
Place of
unorganized and
inefficient activity

Forest:
General Picture
Group of People

Garden:
New Place of
Ministry

High Rise Building:
Prophetic Church
Great Revelation
Fast Growth

Hospital:
Church with
Healing Ministry
Wounded Church
that needs healing
Place of caring,
love and rest

Hotel, Motel:
Churches together
within a City
Place of rest
Communion
Temporary
Situation
Transition
Staying
Temporary

House:
The Church
Your House
Your Body
Your Family
Home Church

Related to the House:

Attic:
Of the Spirit
Spirit Realm
Stored Memories
Thoughts
Attitudes
Learning
Training

Basement:
Storage area
Memories
Past Experiences
Hidden sins
Carnal nature
Lust, Flesh
Thoughts
Attitudes
Sins of
Forefathers
Iniquities hidden

Bathroom:
Deliverance
Ministry
Cleansing, Purging
Healing
Repentance
Confession of Sin
Healing Ministry

Bedroom:
Rest, Privacy
Intimacy
Covenant, Union
Dream and Vision
Ministry
Resting in God
Transition
Slumber, Laziness

Den, Family Room:
Relaxed
Fellowship
Small Groups
Ministry

Dining Room:
Communion
Table of the Lord
Breaking Bread
Fellowship with
Brethren
Teaching and
Preaching to
people

Garage:
Storage
Protection
Outreach Ministry
Missions

Kitchen:
Training
Equipping
Mentoring
Teaching Ministry
Evangelistic
Ministry
The Heart
Spiritual Hunger

Living Room:
Place of fellowship
for family, friends
Church
Small Groups

New House:
New Birth
Change
Transition
New Move
Revival
Healthy Home
New Beginning

Old House:
Old Man
Old ways
Old Mindsets
Past
Inheritance
Home and Church
Old Wineskin
Poverty

Roof:
Covering
Protection
Authority
Thoughts

Heavenly
Revelation

Two Story House:
Two Ministries
Dual Ministry
Spirit and Flesh
Second Level in
Personal Ministry
Revelation
Ground Level:
Of the Flesh
Upper Level:
Of the Spirit

Island:
Alone
Isolated
Church Group

Jungle:
Entanglement
Confusion
Competition
Survival
Danger

Lake, Pond, Pools:
Need Cleansing
Not fresh
Standing Water
Stagnated
Tranquil
Truth, Revelation

Land:
Cleared Land:
New Ministry
Responsive Heart
Neglected Land:
Not responding to
God's Call
No conviction of
the Holy Spirit
Uncaring

Library:
Research in Word
Knowledge Stored
Abundance of
knowledge in
Word
Ministry Research

Motor Home, House Trailer:
Temporary
Church,
Home
Relationship
Situation
Mobile Ministry
Transient

Mountain:
New Heights in
the Spirit
Obstruction
Opposition
Trial
Temptation
The Church
Zion

Multiple Level Building:
Apostolic Church
Great growth
Deeper Truths
Strong Foundation

Park:
Play, Enjoying
Family
Enjoying God
Worship
Peace, rest,
refreshing
Entertainment

Pier, Jetty, Wharf:
Place of Launching
Place of Equipping
Missions Base of
Operations

Prison:
Bondage
Rebellion
Lawlessness
Persecution
Hell
Slavery
Lost Souls

Restaurant (Fast Food):
Unhealthy Church
False Teaching
No Nourishment

Popular
Superficial
Repetitive Ministry
or works

Restaurant:
Church with
Teaching Ministry
Mentoring Ministry
Discipleship
Ministry
Good or bad food

River:
The Word of Truth
Clean River:
Good Teaching
Revelation
Revival
Spiritual Renewal
Dirty River:
Deception
False Teaching
Compromise

Road, Path:
Way or Direction
of Your Life
Rough Road:
Trials, tests
Neglected Road:
Laziness, apathy
Narrow Road:
Difficulty ahead
Blocked Road:
Opposition ahead
in your present
path

School:
Church
Place of Teaching,
Preparation,
Mentoring,
Discipleship,
Equipping,
Training,
Teaching Ministry

Sea, Ocean:
People, Nations
State of the
Peoples or Nations

VEHICLES

Airplane:
Ministry flowing in heavenly Realm
Powerful Ministry
Ministry flying too high or too low

Bicycle:
Young or Immature Ministry
Mobile Ministry
Able to maneuver and go where others cannot

Blimp:
Heavy and awkward Ministry
Filled with Pride
Puffed up
Moved by any Wind of Doctrine
Weak
Slow to Move

Boat, Ship:
Local Church Ministry
Sail Boat:
Ministry Totally Relying upon the Holy Spirit
Row Boat:
Ministry doing carnal works of men, flesh
Cruise Ship:
Ministry that entices by and emphasizes Entertainment
Slave Ship:
Ministry that holds people captive or in bondage
Hospital Ship:
Ministry of Healing
War Ship:
Ministry given to warfare through hate, criticism, or subversion
Battleship:
Warfare on a larger scale
Ship:
Large, complex Ministry or Church
Fishing Boat:
Ministry of Evangelism, Discipleship
Barge:
Ministry full of sin and compromise
Over Burdened
Pride
Submarine:
Hidden agendas, being under situations and circumstances
Paddle Boat:
Ministry of the Flesh, Works, No Spirit Leading
Cargo Ship:
Ministry in the Marketplace
Overburdened

Bus:
Sizable Ministry
Group Ministry
School Bus:
Youth Ministry
Church Bus:
Church Ministry
Tour Bus:
Christian sightseer
Not committed
Carnal

Cars:
Car:
Personal Ministry
Convertible:
Ministry of much Revelation
Old Car:
Old Ministry, Ministry operating in the past
New Car:
New Ministry, Ministry operating in the Holy Spirit
Four Wheel Drive:
Ground Breaking Ministry
Car Wreck:
Confrontation
Strife between people in Ministry
Car Wrecking
Junk Yard:
Ministries destroyed by situations
Need Repair, healing

Car Tires:
Flat:
Ministry operating without the Spirit
Big:
Powerful Ministry full of the Holy Spirit Power
Small:
Needs more prayer in Ministry

Other Vehicles, Transportation:
Combine:
Evangelist
Reaper
Intercessor
Glider, Hang Glider:
Ministry totally dependant upon the Holy Spirit
Ministry carried away by every wind of Doctrine
Parachute:
Able to overcome trials and tribulations
Rocket:
Powerful Ministry that goes deep into the Heavenly Realms
Roller Blades, Roller Skates, Skate Board:
Ministry learning

the things of the
Spirit
Young Ministry
Semi:
Large Ministry
Powerful Ministry
Ministry that is
transportable
Carries great
weight
Tractor:
Spiritual Farmer
Seed Sower
Plower in the
Spirit
Intercessor
Train:
Great Move of
God in the earth
Great Work of the
Holy Spirit
Trucks:
Ministry of Helps
Service
Transportation
Van:
Group Ministry
Family Ministry

VARIOUS DIFFERENT ITEMS:

Altar:
Place of Slaughter
Death to Self Life,
Will, Flesh
Consecration
Intercession
Given up to God

Anchor:
Safety
Security
Hope

Ark:
Christ
Refuge
Salvation

Arm:
Power
Strength

Savior
Deliverer
Striker
Judgment
Arm of the Flesh

Armor:
Divine Equipment
for Warfare
Protection
Wrapped in Truth

Arrows, Spears:
Word of God's
Deliverance
Lies, Gossip
Slander
Curses
Bitter Words
Swift, Silent
Attacks
Go forth, go in
this direction

Ashes:
Repentance
Destruction
Death of Self Life
Memories
Mourning

Atomic Bomb:
Last Days Sign
Great Warfare
Sudden
Destruction

Autumn, Fall Season:
Change,
Transition
Repentance
Completion

Axe:
Gospel Preaching
Exhorting
Rebuking
Getting to the root
of the problem

Balances, Weights:
Being Weighed
Justice
Judgment
Honesty or
Dishonesty

Balance or
Imbalance
Separation

Balm, Oil:
Healing,
Restoration
Healing Ministry
Healing Anointing
Holy Spirit
Jesus-Balm of
Gilead

Banner, Flag:
The Word
Our Standard
Truth Lifted Up
Warfare

Baptism:
Death of Flesh Life
Death of Old Life
Covenant
Cleansing
Immersed
Initiation

Bells:
Change
Warning
God's Presence

Belly:
Seat of Emotions
Spirit pours out of
belly as a river
Love
Innermost Part

Binoculars, Field Glasses, Telescope, Periscope:
Clarity
Focused Vision
Future Event
Inspection
Look Closer
Prophetic Vision
Revealing
Uncovering
Unveiling

Blood:
Change
Covenant
Deliverance

Grace
Guilt
Life of the Flesh
Murder
Redemption
Unclean or defiled

Bones:
Spiritual condition
of the Church
Spiritual condition
of the heart
Death

Book:
The Word
Learning
Teaching
Divine Revelation
Knowledge
Book of Life
Book of
Remembrance

Bow:
Might
Deliverance
Judgment
Accusations
Lies
Gossip
Slander
Prayer

Branches:
God's People
Churches
Victory

Bread:
Word of God
Doctrine
Teaching
Communion
Provision

Brick:
False Stone
Slavery
Works of man

Bridge:
Bridge between
man and God
Faith
Jesus Christ
Peace

Support
The Cross
Unity

Candle:
Light
Revelation
Spirit of Man
Spirit of God
Truth
Word of God

**Chain, Rope,
Cord:**
Captivity
Bondage
Means for taking
Captive
Unity
Agreement

Chair, Seat:
Position
Receiving
Rest
Waiting

Chaff:
Carnality
False
Flesh
Sin
Useless
Will Be Burned
Works of Flesh

Circle:
Completeness
Covenant
Divine Purpose
Endless
Eternal
Whole

Clay:
Human Flesh
People
Earthly
Weakness

Clock:
Timing
Delay
Transition
Time running out
Time speeding up
God's Timing

Clouds:
Coming Storm
Presence of God
Glory of God
Chariots of God
Covering of God
Angels

Crossroads:
Change
Transition
Decision
Choices to be
made
New Direction
Job Change

Dam:
Obstruction to the
Power of God
Block
Reserve
Obstacle
Great Power

Darkness:
Ignorance
Deception
Unbelief
Death
Sorrow
Distress
Destruction
Judgment
Curse
Blindness

**Daytime,
Daylight:**
Truth
Light
Evil Uncovered
Blessings
Sight
Goodness
Purity

Death:
Final Separation
from God in Hell
Spiritual Death
Natural Death
The End
Termination
Loss
Sorrow

Repentance
Consecration

Diamond:
Valuable and
Precious
Gift of the Spirit
Costly
Hard
Hardness
Hard headed
Unchanging
Cuts anything
Multi-Faceted

**Dreaming In a
Dream:**
Message within a
message
A deep Spiritual
Truth
A Vision

Drowning:
Overcome
Depression
Pity
Grief
Sorrow
Temptation
Backslid
Excessive Debt
Problems
Overwhelming
Crisis handled in
the flesh
Stress
Pressure
Compromise
Needing Attention

Ear:
Hearing
Listening
Discerning
Faith comes by
Hearing

Earthquake:
Judgment
Shaking of God
Vibration
Upheaval
Change by Crisis
Trauma
Disaster

Shock
Repentance

Egypt:
World
Worldliness
Bondage
Idolatry
Slavery
Captivity

Electricity:
Power of the Holy
Spirit
Authority
Prayer

**Escalator,
Elevator:**
People
Ministries going in
the same direction
Working together
Rising up in Spirit
Revelation
Falling away
Going deeper
Regressing into
the works flesh

Explosion:
Sudden Expansion
Increase
Growth
Swift Change
Destruction
Judgment
Revelation
Revival
Healings En-
masse

Eyes:
Sight
Seeing
Understanding
Desire for good or
evil
Covetous
Passion
Lust
Greed
Flirting
Cunning
Insight
Foresight

Knowledge
Window of Soul
Eyes on the
Cherubim
The Eyes of God
All seeing
All knowing God
Closed Eyes:
Unbelief
Sleeping
Apathy
Open Eyes:
Understanding
Discerning
Alert Aware

Face:
Character of
person
Their heart
Image
Nature
Mood

Falling:
Falling away from
God
Falling into sin
No Support
No Foundation
Trial
Temptation
Demotion

Feathers:
Covering
Spiritual Covering
Freedom
Angels

Feet:
Your Walk,
Calling,
Heart,
Thoughts,
Conduct
Bare Feet:
No Spiritual
Preparation
Unsaved
Easily Offended
Tender
No burden for
Lost or Hurting

Fire:
Trial
Heat
Burden
Persecution
Hate
Anger
Sacrifice
Dedication
Fleshly Desire
Lust
Passion for Christ
Devotion
Judgment
Purifying
Testing
Presence of God
Pillar of Fire
Calling
Invitation
Commissioning
Angels
Messengers of
Fire
Chariots of Fire
Whirlwind of Fire
Cherubims come
out of God's Fire
Powerful Power of
God Released
Revival
Word shut up
within you

Flood:
Judgment
Deluge
Overpowering
Overwhelm
Confusion
Temptation
Depression
Accusations
Lies
Flood of Filth
Flood of Unrest
Flood of Memories
Regrets

Fog:
Confusion,
Compromise
Deception
Deceit

Doctrines of men
Clouded Thoughts
Uncertainty

Forehead:
Rebellion
Strong Willed
Thoughts
Reasoning
Mind
Imagination
Memories
Firm in Stance

Furnace:
Heat
Trial
Testing
Purifying
Purging
Refining
The Heart
Anger
Wrath
Judgment
Death
Suffering
Persecution for
the faith

Garbage, Trash:
Unclean
Vile
Rotten
Defilement
Corruption
False Doctrines
Teachings
Gossip
Slander
Weights and
Burdens people
place upon you
Unbelief
Carnality

Gasoline, Fuel:
Prayer
Power of the Spirit
Gossip
Slander
Contention
Strife
False Doctrines
False Accusations

Gate, Portal, Port:
Jesus Christ, The
Gate through
which all men will
pass unto God
Place of Business
Place of Healing
Place of Judgment
and Justice
Place where
Power flows into
or out of
Praise
The Cross
The 5 Senses
Trade
Thanksgiving
Entrance to:
Church
City
City of God
Family
Heart
Heaven
Hell
Jerusalem
Nation
Presence of God
Spirit Realm
State
Throne Room

Grass:
Carnality
Spiritual Condition
of the Heart
The Flesh
The Word

Guns, Bullets:
Accusations
Authority
Curses
Envy
Gossip
Malice
Murder
Power
Rage
Revenge
Slander
Warfare
Words

Hail:
Burning
Hail of Fire
Judgment
Divine Hail
Natural Hail
Weather
Punishment
Bombarded by the
enemy

Hair:
*Long Hair in
Women:*
Authority
Covering
Glory
Protection
Tradition
*Short Hair in
Women:*
Carnality
Homosexuality
Rebellion
Sin Nature
Uncovered
Unprotected
Un-submissive
Long Hair in Men:
Carnality
Effeminate
Homosexuality
Lawlessness
Rebellion
Sin Nature
Un-submissive
Short Hair in Men:
Manliness
Order
Respect

Haircut:
Breaking of:
Consecration
Covenant
Traditions
Covering
Vows

Hammer:
Break
Destruct
Pound
Preach
Shatter

Word of God

Hand:
Action
Clean Hands
Good or Bad Deed
Heart Revealed
Idolatry
Service
Spiritual Warfare
Surrender
Worship
Works of the Flesh
Right Hand:
Faithfulness
Honor
Power of God
Strength
Left Hand:
Dark
Deceit
Dishonor
Hidden
Sinister
Unclean
Hand Missing:
Death
Severe Judgment
Fingers Missing:
Judgment,
Severity depends
on the number of
missing fingers

Harp:
Worship
Lust
Symbol of Lust
Deliverance (*while
harp is playing*)

Head:
Authority
Covering
Husband
Intelligence
Knowledge Lord
Leadership
Mind
Pastor
Power
Ruler
Thoughts
Wisdom

Hips:
Birthing
Enticements
Joints
Loins
Lust (*Swinging
Hips*)
Mind
Offenses
Reproduction
Truth

Horn, Trumpet:
Announcement
Call to Attention
Call to Action
Declaration
New Season
Power
Revelation Given
Strength
Summons
War

Jewel, Jewelry:
Betrothal
Covenant
Gifted Person
Precious
People of God
Pride
Treasure
Truth

Keys:
Christ
Faith
Important
Key of David
Authority to:
Bind and Loose
Open and Shut
Key to:
Death, Hell and
Grave
Kingdom
Bottomless Pit
Revelation
Truth
Understanding
Wisdom

Kiss:
Agreement
Betrayal

Brother
Covenant
Deceit
Friend
Lust
Seduction

Knees:
Obedience
Rebellion
Reverence
Submission
Surrender
Unyielding
Worship

Knives, Swords:
Angry rebuke
Accusation
Curses
Gossip
Judgment
Revelation
Slander
Sword of Spirit
and Truth
The Word
Weapon
Warfare

Ladder, Stairs, Steps:
Ascend or
Descend
Demotion
Entrance or
Escape
Promotion or
Portal
Struggle if hard to
climb up

Lamp, Candle:
Illumination
Revelation
Spirit of God
Spirit of man
Truth
Word of God

Leaven, Leprosy:
Cleansed by
Burning or
Removal from
within

Death
Defilement
False Doctrine
Pride
Sin
Self
Uncleanness
Zeal

Lips:
Covenant
Enticements
Honor
Integrity
Life or Death in
the Words spoken
forth
Promise
Seduction
Truth
Word
Word of your
Testimony

Manna:
Creative Miracles
Divine Counsel
Divine Provision
Jesus, the Bread
of Life
Living Word
Revelation
Preaching of the
Rhema Word
Spirit of Truth
Truth
Understanding
Wisdom
Word of God

Map:
Advice
Correction
Direction
Instruction
Mandates
New Assignment
New Task Given
to You
Strategies
Plans
Summons

Microphone, Loud Speaker:
Authority
Declaration
Decree in the
Heavenlies
Prophetic Voice
Voice of God

Moon:
Apostate
Church
Emotions
False
Feminine
Harvest time
Judgment Coming
Light in Darkness
Man
Occult
Persecution
Season Change
Sign of the Son of
Witchcraft
War Coming

Name, Title:
Character
Position
Prophetic Symbol
Reputation
Respect
Reverence
Title

Neck:
Arrogance
Authority
Hard-Headed
Hard Hearted
Proud
Rebellion
Rule
Self-Will
Stubbornness
Strength
Stiff Necked

North:
Heaven
Home of God
Judgment
Majesty
Power
Warfare

Perfume, Aroma, Scent:
Aroma of Christ
Aroma of the
Prayers of the
Saints
Deception
Discernment
Enticements
Influence
Lily of the Valley
Love
Memorial
Perfume
Persuasion
Rose of Sharon
Seduction
Temptation
The Holy Spirit

Pillar:
Courage
Fearless
Strength
Support
Foundational truth
Wisdom
Pillar of Truth
Pillar of Fire

Plow:
Breaking open
Call
Fallow ground
Not fit for
Kingdom when
you look back
Preparation for
sowing
Rejecting God's
service
Uncovering the
hard heart
Work for God

Plumb Line:
Divine Balance
Holiness
Judgment
Standard
Justice
Measuring
Weighed in the
The Word

Sackcloth:
Fasting
Judgment
Mourning
Sorrow
Repentance

Salt:
Believers of the
earth
Cleansing
Covenant
Flavor
Healing
Incorruptible Life
Preservation
Purging

Sand:
Generations
Inheritance
Irritation
Memorial
Multitudes
Pillar of Salt
Relatives
Sea of Salt
Seed of Abraham
Time
Unsaved people in
the earth

Scepter:
Acceptance
Authority
Throne Entrance
Favor with King
Power
Promotion
Rule
Reign

Shoulder:
Authority
Bare Shoulders:
Seduction
Burden Bearing
Carry the Ark
Covenant Rights
Droopy Shoulder:
depressed, tired
discouraged
Government
Responsibility
Rulership

Strength
Stubborn
Temptation
Truth

Shovel:
Ask about
Bury
Confession
Declarations
Dig
Gossip
Inquire of
Prayer
Search for
Slander
Tongue
Uncover

Sleep:
Apathy
Danger
Death
Ignorant
Indifference
Laziness
Rest
Slumber
Spiritual Death
Transition
Unaware
Waiting

Star:
Announcement
Apostle
Christ
Daystar Arising
Healing
Heavenly seed
Heavens
Israel
Ministers of God
Sign in the
The Church

Stone, Rock:
False Witness
Foundation
Jesus Christ
Judgment
Name of Saints on
a white stone
Persecution
Stable

Strength
The Word
Urim & Thummim
Witness

Storm:
Anger
Coming Attack
Destruction
Distress
Disturbance
Enemy's Power
God's Power
Judgment
Persecution
Rage
Sudden Calamity
Trouble
Warfare

**Suit Case,
Baggage:**
Burdens you carry
around
Change
Compromise
Personal Property
Relocate
Temporary
Travel
Sins that are not
dealt with
Your Heart

Sweeping:
Change
Cleaning
Debris
Intercession
Obstacles
Rebuking
Removing
Repentance
Spiritual Warfare

Swimming:
Flowing in Spirit
Gifts of the Spirit
God
Moving Deeper
Partaking of Truth
Prophesying
Revelation
Serving God
Spiritual Activity

Utter Surrender
Worshipping

Telephone:
Communication
Counsel
Enemy's voice
Gossip
Intercession
Message from God
New
Prayer
Prayer hindered
Prophetic Decrees
Revelation
Speaking to you

**Tent of Meeting,
Tabernacle,
Temple:**
Body of Christ
Christ among us
Devotion
Emmanuel
Fellowship
Full of the Spirit
God
God's dwelling
Holiness
Holy of Holies
Intimacy with God
Place of Worship
Purity
Sanctuary
Temple Worship
Yielded to God
Your Spirit
Your Body
Your Soul

Thunder:
Blessings
Communion
Change of Age
Judgment
Not understanding
what the Spirit is
saying
Prophetic Decrees
Shut up
Voice of God
Warning of
judgment to come

Urinating:
Cleansing
Compelling Urge
Curses
Defilement
Enmity
Offenses
Pressure
Purification
Rebellion
Release
Repentance
Temptation

Veil:
Bride
Christ, the Veil
that was rent for
men
Concealment
Covering over
bed, head
Deception
Flesh
Glory
God
Hiddenness
New Beginnings
Portal
Release
Revelation
Salvation when
parted, and
removed
Separation
That which
divides, separates
The Train of God
Veil of the heart
removed
Veil over the
minds removed

Volcano:
Anger
Demonic Release
Emotionally
unstable
Eruption
Hate
Murder
Persecution
Pressure Release
Rage

Sudden Calamity
Swift Judgment
Trials
Trouble
Unpredictable
Violence

Wilderness:
Barrenness
Empowerment
Confusion
Intercession
Life without God
Place of:
Testing
Refining
Training
Equipping
Temptation
Wandering

Wind:
Breath of Life
Destruction
Doctrines: False
or True
Four Winds of
Heaven
Idle Words
Opposition
Power of God
Revelation
Season Change
Spirits
Storms
Wind of the Spirit

Wood:
Building Material
Carnality
Flesh
Humanity
Life
The Cross
Works of men

Yoke:
Bondage
Equal or Unequal
Fellowship
Forced Labor
Mentoring
Relationship
Servant
Service

Slavery
Suffering
Surrender
Training
Total Union

Zeal:
Commitment
Devoted Service
Energy
Force
Forceful Love
Misdirected
Passion for God
Strong Emotion
Total allegiance
Wholly Devoted